GREAT MYSTERIES

Witches

OPPOSING VIEWPOINTS®

Look for these and other exciting *Great Mysteries: Opposing Viewpoints* books:

GREAT MYSTERIES

Witches

OPPOSING VIEWPOINTS®

by Wendy Stein

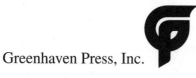

Greenhaven Press, Inc.   P.O. Box 289009, San Diego, California 92198-9009

Library of Congress Cataloging-in-Publication Data

Stein, Wendy.
    Witches : opposing viewpoints / by Wendy Stein.
        p. cm. — (Great mysteries)
    Includes bibliographical references and index.
    ISBN 1-56510-240-1   (alk. paper)
    1. Witchcraft—Juvenile literature.   [1. Witchcraft.]
    I. Title.   II. Series: Great mysteries (Saint Paul, Minn.)
    BF1566.S772   1995
    133.4'3—dc20
                                                94-26531
                                                  CIP
                                                     AC

34,040 ✗

For MaryAnn—finally!

Contents

Introduction

This book is written for the curious—those who want to explore the mysteries that are everywhere. To be human is to be constantly surrounded by wonderment. How do birds fly? Are ghosts real? Can animals and people communicate? Was King Arthur a real person or a myth? Why did Amelia Earhart disappear? Did history really happen the way we think it did? Where did the world come from? Where is it going?

Great Mysteries: Opposing Viewpoints books are intended to offer the reader an opportunity to explore some of the many mysteries that both trouble and intrigue us. For the span of each book, we want the reader to feel that he or she is a scientist investigating the extinction of the dinosaurs, an archaeologist searching for clues to the origin of the great Egyptian pyramids, a psychic detective testing the existence of ESP.

One thing all mysteries have in common is that there is no ready answer. Often there are *many* answers but none on which even the majority of authorities agrees. *Great Mysteries: Opposing Viewpoints* books introduce the intriguing views of the experts, allowing the reader to participate in their explorations, their theories, and their disagreements as they try to explain the mysteries of our world.

But most readers won't want to stop here. These *Great Mysteries: Opposing Viewpoints* aim to stimulate the reader's curiosity. Although truth is often impossible to discover, the search is fascinating. It is up to the reader to examine the evidence, to decide whether the answer is there—or to explore further.

"Penetrating so many secrets, we cease to believe in the unknowable. But there it sits nevertheless, calmly licking its chops."

H.L. Mencken, American essayist

Preface

What Is a Witch?

When you hear the word *witch*, what comes to mind? To many people, one of the most common images of the witch is the Wicked Witch of the West, from *The Wizard of Oz*. She is old, ugly, and dressed in black from her cone-shaped hat to her pointed shoes. She carries a broom, and on command, it can whisk her away, high above the ground. She cackles wickedly and incites fear wherever she goes. When she points her long, deformed finger and recites her evil curses, her enemies face doom.

The witch of the fairy tale *Hansel and Gretel* was another ugly and vicious woman. She sent a lovely bird to lure the tired, hungry children to her. Using magic, she created a house of bread with a roof made of cake, and when the children stopped to eat, she invited them inside. She tricked Hansel and Gretel with her kindness, then took them prisoner. Her plan was to fatten them up—then eat them.

But images of good witches also inhabit fairy tales. The beautiful Glinda in *The Wizard of Oz* could grant a wish with a wave of her wand. She did not need to ride a broom; she traveled in a sphere of light. All kindness and beauty, she seemed almost like a goddess. She and the Wicked Witch of the

(Opposite page) The image of the witch that comes quickest to everyone's mind is the old, evil, addled crone—no more perfectly portrayed than in the film *The Wizard of Oz*.

West stood in stark contrast to one another: pure goodness versus pure evil. One practiced helpful magic, the other harmful magic.

Were these witches only fictional characters, the results of vivid imaginations? Actually, the wicked witch of fairy tales, movies, and Halloween evolved from the fears and superstitions of people who lived in Europe many hundreds of years ago.

The image of the good witch also has its roots in ancient days, when people believed that folk healers and midwives performed magic to cure disease and assist in childbirth. Both images—the good witch and the wicked witch—show the power and nature

In stark contrast to the Wicked Witch of the West was Glinda, the good witch, also portrayed in *The Wizard of Oz*. Both images had their roots in ancient times.

of magical belief; magic can destroy or heal, depending upon the witch's intent.

Witches Were Magicians

Long ago, witches were simply considered sorcerers or magicians. They used magic and were in touch with supernatural powers. Many people thought that bad things happened because of witches' evil spells. But they believed that other witches could provide protection from or remedies for those spells.

A witch shoots a twig through a man's foot. Once Christianity became widespread, superstitions about witches' evil powers abounded.

The practice of magic was an important part of pagan religions. Pagan religions existed long before Judaism, Christianity, or Islam. They date back to the Stone Age. For thousands of years people worshipped many nature gods or believed that spirits inhabited trees, rocks, the sky, the water, and all other things.

Within a few centuries of the death of Jesus, Christianity became the official religion throughout much of Europe. Although many people continued to believe in their pagan traditions, the Church and early governments started to outlaw pagan and magical practices. Early Christians considered anyone who followed pre-Christian traditions to be uncivilized. They used the word *pagan* as an insult. And they perceived anyone who continued to use magic as a threat to Christianity and to the state. Magical use of herbs, spell-casting, healing with magic, and foretelling the future became suspicious activities. Observing pagan festivals or worshipping pagan gods became a crime. Many Christian leaders thought that people who practiced magic and pagan religion were undermining the authority of the church and God by calling upon spirits or gods other than the One Christian God. To the church, all pre-Christian gods or spirits were false gods and therefore evil. Witches and others who continued to worship pre-Christian deities (gods) must therefore be in league with the devil, the agent of evil. The church accused witches of all sorts of diabolical activities— flying, sacrificing and eating babies, using familiars (spirit guardians in animal form), killing with magic, having sex with the devil, attending secret devilish meetings, and so on.

These loathsome devil worshippers had to be eliminated, the church and governments said. If they were not crushed, they would destroy society. By the fourteenth century, witch hysteria overtook entire regions. People became suspicious of one another. It did not take much evidence to make an accusation. "She looked at me funny, and the next thing I knew, my cow stopped giving milk," someone might say,

A suspected witch is arrested during the witch trials in Salem, Massachusetts. The hunt for witches bordered on hysteria.

and a neighbor would be carted off to jail. Between the fourteenth and eighteenth centuries, hundreds of thousands of people were executed.

The witch hysteria was not limited to Europe. English Puritans who journeyed to the New World brought with them the old fears of magic and the devil. The witch hysteria broke out occasionally in colonial New England, too.

The witch hysteria finally ended in the eighteenth century in both Europe and America. Since that time, historians have wondered: Why did this happen? Did the accused people really worship the devil? Did they practice evil magic? Or were they simply innocent victims or scapegoats for the problems of their communities?

What Does *Witch* Mean?

Just who and what are witches? Witches have existed throughout the world for thousands of years. The understanding of what a witch is varies from culture to culture and also changes with the times. The word *witch* may have positive or negative associations.

The word has been applied to folk healers, midwives, good magicians, evil magicians, shapeshifters, witch doctors, shamans, devil worshippers, goddess worshippers, grave robbers, worshippers of pagan gods, psychics, and fortune-tellers. It has been used in an insulting manner to describe unattractive women, powerful women, eccentric women, even women in general.

The concept of the witch has become tangled over the years until we have a single word that applies to many very diverse traditions and beliefs all over the world. In this book, however, we will be looking at the witches of Europe, Puritan America, and the contemporary United States. But even the witches of these limited places and times are a jigsaw puzzle of beliefs and traditions, in which some of the pieces are missing or just do not fit. Looking

"It is a most certain . . . opinion that there are sorcerers and witches who by the help of the Devil, on account of a compact which they have entered into with him are able . . . to produce real and actual evils and harm."

Jakob Sprenger and Heinrich Kramer, *Malleus Maleficarum*, 1486

"As is often the case, the truth about Witchcraft is far less tantalizing than the lies. It doesn't lend itself as readily to talk shows as Satanism and rarely creates headline news."

Wiccan and author Scott Cunningham, *The Truth About Witchcraft Today*, 1988 at the origins of the word *witch* is a good first step to understanding what a witch is.

The Word *Witch:* Its Meaning and Its Origins

Witch comes from the Old English word *wicca* (pronounced "witcha"), meaning "male witch," and wicce (pronounced "witcheh"), meaning "female witch." The verb *wiccian* meant "to cast a spell," "to work sorcery," or "to bewitch." So a witch is one who casts spells or bewitches others.

Some people also relate the word *wicca* to the Old English words *witan*, meaning "to know," or *wis* meaning "wise." To these people, *witch* means "wise person," and witchcraft is the craft of the wise. But others who study the derivation of words dispute the word's connection to the words *witan* and *wis*.

Writer and poet Erica Jong writes in her 1981 book *Witches* that *witch* might have come from the old Teutonic verb *wik*, meaning "to bend." This would also relate to the use of magic, since magicians—including witches—appear to "bend" nature to suit their purposes.

According to the *American Heritage Dictionary*, *witch* is also related to the Germanic word *wikkjaz*, meaning "necromancer" or "one who wakes the dead." This possibility suggests that witches are associated with the underworld of the dead.

Many modern witches call themselves Wiccans and say that they practice Wicca rather than witchcraft. They adopted these ancient terms because they say that the word *witch* carries too many negative images. Some modern-day witches consider witchcraft a religion. They use the term *wicca* to set them apart from other contemporary witches who primarily consider witchcraft to be the practice of a magic craft.

The word *witch* has many possible meanings,

Witches were thought to be overwhelmingly powerful and to possess an intimate knowledge of nature. In this woodcut, witches create a brew to cause a violent storm.

most of them relating to the unknown, or the supernatural. But however the word is defined, the concept of witchcraft and the image of witches conjure up mystery and magic.

One

What Did People Believe About Witches?

> May you be consumed as coal upon the hearth,
> May you shrink as dung upon a wall,
> and may you dry up as water in a pail.
> May you become as small as a linseed grain,
> and much smaller than the hipbone of an itchmite,
> and may you become so small that you become nothing.
>
> *Anglo-Saxon curse to destroy an enemy*

Once upon a time, people looked upon nature as an awesome and mysterious force. They looked for explanations for the lightning in the sky, floods and storms, illness, birth and death. They concluded that unseen supernatural forces or spirits of nature were at work in the world.

But people despaired to think that they lived in a world beyond their control. They came to believe that certain people—shamans, medicine men and women, sorcerers, witches—could intervene with the mysterious forces that controlled the world. They believed that these people used magic to make things happen—both the good and the bad events of their lives. And so, magic was born—the ability to manipulate unseen forces in order to bring about a desired result.

Magic practice is universal; evidence of magic's use is found in every ancient culture scholars have studied. The earliest clues about the practice of

(Opposite page) In this fanciful illustration, witches terrorize a family with their antics.

A witch terrorizes the countryside by creating a storm. Witches' ability to use herbs and potions made people wonder if they had other, more complete powers.

magic in Europe come from cave drawings at least seventeen thousand years old. Some of these drawings seem to show ancient people using magic to ensure a successful hunt.

Sorcery

Witches in cultures throughout the world knew how to use herbs and other ingredients to concoct potions that could cure many ills. People believed they knew how to cast spells to harm and spells to protect. They were thought to be in touch with the supernatural; they were keepers of magic.

The simplest form of magic is sorcery. Sorcery involves casting a spell through the use of ritual, magical words, and often physical objects to bring about either a harmful or beneficial result.

According to writers Derek and Julia Parker, in *The Power of Magic*, spell-casting "is based on the idea . . . that the known universe is one—that no force exists without being connected to all other forces, and that therefore one force can be made to affect another force." So, earlier people believed that a ceremony could make crops grow, or a spell could bring harm or benefit. In some traditions, scattering blood over a field might ensure a good harvest. Dipping a twig in water and sprinkling the water in the air could bring rain. Witches did not necessarily have to perform the magic themselves. They sold spells and curses to non-witches. The Anglo-Saxon spell that opens this chapter is an example of a sold spell, supposed to destroy an enemy by reducing him to nothing.

Sympathetic Magic

One of the most common types of sorcery is sympathetic, or image, magic. This involves the use of puppets (portraits, dolls, or other images of a person), or perhaps a piece of clothing, a fingernail, or a lock of hair belonging to the person toward whom the magic is directed. For example, people thought a witch could cause death by melting a wax image of a person.

Simple magic was also called folk magic because it was used to affect the everyday lives of the folk—the people. Folk magic was used to improve or block the flow of a cow's milk, to cure or cause illness, to protect or destroy a home. Witches used powders, potions, herbs, incantations, puppets, and other tools to perform their magic.

Before the Christian era, witches in Europe were usually women. They were the village healers and spell-makers. They were both respected and feared because of their awesome powers to bring wealth, love, health, or sickness and death. They were sometimes believed to be able to fly, change shape, talk to animals, or raise spirits. Members of witches' communities came to them with requests. But while they were important to the village, they were usually outsiders. They remained apart from others because of their ability to communicate with spirits and because of their reputed great power. But "the stronger the powers of these outsiders were rumored to be, the more they were persecuted," especially by the authorities, say Derek and Julia Parker.

Christian Belief Changes Witchcraft

As Christianity replaced pagan religions, witches became figures of great suspicion because of their association with pagan spirits. Over the centuries, the tradition of the witch as a folk magician was replaced by the image of the diabolical (devilish) witch. The witches' power did not come from the church, so it did not come from God, Christians believed. Therefore, it must come from the devil. Saint Augustine (354–430) wrote that pagan magic was invented by the devil so that he could tempt humans away from Christ and the truth.

The authorities tended to stimulate the superstitions of the people in order to stir up witch hysteria. From remnants of pagan belief, some historians charge, the Inquisition (judicial proceedings begun by the church in the thirteenth century to combat heresy, or challenges to the church) built a distorted picture of witches and their practices. The years from 1450 to 1700 became known as the Burning Times because so many women and men were burned at the stake for allegedly indulging in devil-worshipping practices, including flight, sabbats (witches' ceremonial gatherings), initiations, and association with animal demons known as familiars.

The Flight of the Witch

During the period of the witch-hunts, people believed that witches could fly, on broomstick, fork, or shovel, in a sieve, or on some other vehicle. Some witches were said to ride demons that had taken the shapes of goats, cows, or other animals.

The belief in the ability to fly has been a long-standing and important aspect of many spiritual traditions. Flying represents the freedom of the spirit or soul to break away from the physical world and travel in the spirit world. Sorcerers, shamans, medicine men and women, yogis, and other spiritual figures have all claimed to be able to fly. These various spiritual figures achieve their flying state through a variety of mind-altering practices, such as meditation, dancing, drumming, chanting, and using halucinogenic drugs or ointments.

Despite the long tradition of flying mystics, by the tenth century most educated people in Europe were skeptical of this ability. The *Canon Episcopi* was a document issued by the Roman Catholic

Many people believed that witches had the power to fly. During periods of witch-hunts, many women were tortured until they confessed to having flown with the devil.

Church in around A.D. 900. It asserted that witches flew only in their own imaginations. Nevertheless, in the fifteenth century, church authorities were anxious for excuses to prosecute witches. They again promoted tales of the flying witch. According to the *Malleus Maleficarum,* a fifteenth-century witch-hunters' guide, a German priest actually saw a man picked up and carried through the air by an invisible force.

Under torture, many accused witches confessed that they had flown to meetings with the help of demons. A few alleged witches even confessed willingly. Isobel Gowdie, tried for witchcraft in Scotland in 1662, actually turned herself in. Records of her voluntary confession contain her description of her night flights:

> We take our windle-straws or beanstalks and put them between our feet and say thrice, "Horse and hattock, Horse and pellatis, ho!" and immediately we fly to wherever we would. We fly like straws when we please. If anyone sees our straws in a whirlwind and does not bless himself, we may shoot him dead at our pleasure.

Her willingness to confess to flying and all sorts of other witch activities cast doubt on her testimony—even during her own time. Some authorities thought she was insane.

Testing a Witch's Claims

Some witches confessed they could fly physically, while others said they flew in spirit. Sometimes, the accused witch did not seem to know the difference. One woman testified that she had been flying to witches' gatherings every night—even though she had been locked in a prison cell. Authorities tested her story through observation. They saw her lie down on her bed and become rigid. Doctors and other officials then entered the room and pinched her to try to awaken her. When that failed, they burned the soles of her feet with a candle. Still she did not awaken. When she finally woke up, she told the details of the sabbat she had attended. Her body had never left the room, but she swore she had been at a sabbat and did not even feel the pain in her feet until she awoke.

Records from witch trials and legends from the time of the witch-hunts tell of witches using ointments to help them fly. According to popular belief, witches brewed ointments in their cauldrons (large pots). The flying ointments were made from herbs and vile ingredients such as bat's blood and even baby's fat. The witches smeared the ointment on themselves or on their brooms or flying sticks and were transported to gatherings of witches, known as sabbats. Apparently, witches and others believed the ointment helped them to fly physically.

Doubts About Flight

Some brave skeptics from the period of the witch-hunts doubted that physical flight occurred. They maintained that the ointment affected the user's brain and made her think she was flying.

Scientists today speculate that the ointments contained hallucinogenic herbs, which were absorbed through the skin and induced the sensation of flying. Various flying ointment recipes remain from the period. They list ingredients such as aconite, belladonna, hemlock, cannabis, henbane, and other substances that can cause dizziness, irregular heartbeat, confusion, delirium, and hallucinations—such as the sensation of flying.

In recent years, two scientists in Germany actually made a medieval flying ointment and tested it on themselves. They fell into a trancelike sleep for almost an entire day. During their sleep, they both felt they had flown to the top of a mountain to a gathering of demons.

Familiars

Another common belief was that witches had familiars. Authorities claimed that the familiar was

"Sorcerers or witches are the Devil's whores who steal milk, raise storms, ride on goats or broomsticks, lame or maim people, torture babies in their cradles, change things into different shapes."

Protestant Reformation leader Martin Luther, sermon, 1521

"It is strange that we should suppose, that such persons can work such feats: and it is more strange, that we will imagine that to be possible to be done by a witch, which to nature and sense is impossible."

Author Reginald Scot, *The Discoverie of Witchcraft*, 1584

a demon or agent of the devil—or even the devil himself—transformed into animal form to do a witch's evil bidding. People believed familiars could change shape or become invisible.

Familiars were usually small animals such as dogs, cats, toads, mice, and owls. The belief that the devil could appear as a cat or dog made anyone eccentric enough to have a pet a natural suspect. (Few people kept pets in those days.)

Officials also watched for any small animal or insect that went anywhere near an accused witch. During the infamous witch trials in Salem, Massachusetts, in 1692, when a fly buzzed near a defendant, the court concluded that the fly was her familiar.

It was said that in return for their devilish help, the witch fed the familiar her own blood, which the familiar sucked from the witch's skin, leaving a mark. Witch-hunters in Scotland and England were

A witch stands in a magic circle and conjures up imps and familiars in this seventeenth-century woodcut. The accusers of a suspected witch became suspicious of a woman's pets, even insects that alighted upon her, believing these to be her familiars.

the most obsessed with familiars, but throughout Europe, officials searched for witch's marks on the bodies of the accused. Investigators frequently claimed that warts, birthmarks, unusual freckles, extra nipples, red spots, or even bumps under the tongue were witch's marks.

Many witches' familiars had unusual names. Some identified in various witch trials included Grizel, Greedigut, Pyewackett, and Elemauzer. One witch confessed to owning five familiars: Holt, a kitten; Jamara, a spaniel with no legs; Sack and Sugar, a black rabbit; Newes, a polecat; and Vinegar Tom, an animal with a hound's body and an ox's head.

According to twentieth-century historian Jeffrey Russell, the idea of familiars developed from lore about dwarves, fairies, trolls, and other small spirits in northern European tradition. Familiars were originally considered nature spirits. Many were friendly spirits and performed benevolent deeds. The concept of the familiar is still found in many cultures that practice magic. Native American shamans, for example, are said to travel to the spirit world with animal companions.

To church authorities during the witch-hunts, familiars were demons, because the only spiritual entities that could exist, according to the church, were God, angels, the devil, and demons.

Sabbat

Witches were often loners and outcasts. Yet one of the most prominent charges against them was that they participated in a communal and often raucous activity—the witches' sabbat. Accused women and men were tortured and threatened until they confessed that they had attended these celebrations. The image of the sabbats seemed to be a blend of pagan festivals and church propaganda about secret, obscene rites with the devil.

The term *sabbat*, like the English word *sabbath*, may have come from the Hebrew *shabbath*, "to rest."

This illustration depicts a witches' sabbat, where witches would supposedly frolic together and commune with the devil. Most of the surviving accounts of sabbats come from the Inquisition and were solicited under torture.

Many historians speculate that the word was used in an anti-Semitic manner, comparing the witches' allegedly indecent gatherings with the Jews' sacred day of rest and worship. Before adopting the term *sabbat*, the church had also used the Jewish term *synagogue* to refer to the devil-worshipping gatherings it accused its enemies of attending. Its enemies were people of other religions and heretics. Heretics were people who questioned the teachings of the church or broke away from the church.

Some scholars suggest that *sabbat* comes from the French *s'ébattre*, meaning "to frolic"; or from the ancient Babylonian *sa-bat*, meaning "heart rest"; or from the Greek *sabaoth*, meaning "armies" or "hosts."

Official accounts of witches' sabbats did not seem to exist before the fourteenth century, when the Inquisition was in full swing. The idea that heretics met in groups was originally a charge the church leveled at other heretics. In 1022, in Orléans, France, when a group of heretics was tried and executed, the accusations included secret gatherings, sex orgies, child sacrifice, and invoking evil spirits.

Most of our information about the sabbat comes from confessions given during torture. The word was first used in an Inquisition trial in 1335 in Toulouse, France. Accused witch Catherine Delort testified that at sabbats she and others devoured the bodies of children. Ann Marie de Georgel, another accused Toulouse witch, said she had been practicing witchcraft for twenty years. She testified that at the sabbat a male goat taught her spells and showed her how to make poisonous ointments. She gathered ingredients from the clothing, hair, nails, and fat of bodies buried in cemeteries or hanging at gallows.

Devil Worship

According to Inquisition records, the sabbat festivities were centered around the worship of Satan. Male and female witches were said to meet at night in remote places such as forests, mountaintops, or caves. To reach the sabbat, the witches flew, of course, aboard brooms, sticks, or demons in animal guise. Their familiars often accompanied them, too. The devil often arrived in the form of a smelly goat, toad, crow, or black cat, trial transcripts said. The sabbat began with the devil or his representative questioning the attendees on the harmful deeds they had committed since the last meeting. The witches were also required to pay their respects to him with the "kiss of shame," kissing the devil on the buttocks.

After this greeting, witches supposedly took part in a processional and a circle dance. Some historians suggest that Inquisition officials were eager to associate dancing with devil worship since it had

"To attempt to give a description of the Sabbat is to attempt a description of what does not exist and what has never existed save in the fantastic and disordered imagination of warlocks and witches. The pictures which have been drawn of these assemblies are merely the fantasy of those who dreamed they had actually been borne, body and soul, through the air to the Sabbat."

French priest Dom Augustin Calmet, 1761

"Unfortunately the Sabbat did—and does—take place; formerly in deserted wasteland, on the hill-side, in secluded spots, now, as often as not, in the privacy of vaults and cellars, and in those lone empty houses innocently placarded 'To Be Sold.'"

Judge Henri Boguet, seventeenth century

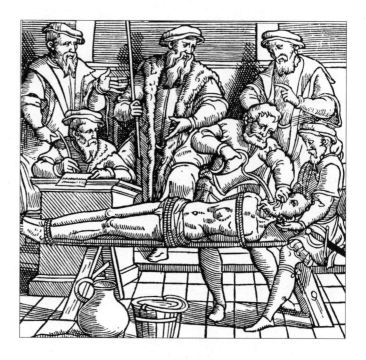

An accused witch is tortured by members of the Inquisition. This witch is being given the water torture: a tube is fed down the throat while a man holds the nose. Victims felt as though they were drowning, as indeed they were.

After greeting the devil, witches supposedly engaged in a circle dance.

been an important part of pagan ritual. The church had banned dancing at celebrations of saints' days.

Accused witches testified that following the dances, a sexual orgy occurred among witches, demons, and the devil himself. Although the Bible described the devil as a fallen angel and neither male nor female, church teaching portrayed the devil as male, and Inquisition records claimed that women had intercourse with him. This accusation more firmly established the idea that witches were likely to be women, although some men were accused of witchcraft as well. The church taught that women were morally weak and easily tempted by the devil.

The sabbat ended with great feasting, but the food was disgusting and inedible to non-witches, according to some reports. Participants drank blood, black moss-water, and wine and ate foods filled with drugs. Witch-hunter Pierre de Lancre said the food served at sabbats included decaying and rotten meat and the flesh of people who had been hanged. He said the witches "banqueted on babies' limbs and toads." They ate and drank themselves into a frenzy, he said. Other witnesses, however, disagreed and pronounced the food very fine and plentiful.

After the meal, the participants flew home. But sometimes they made trouble on the way. Their sabbat magic sank ships, destroyed homes and crops, and killed people and animals. Despite all this troublemaking, witches always arrived home before the sun rose.

Sabbats: A Fabrication?

Rosemary Ellen Guiley writes in the *Encyclopedia of Witches and Witchcraft:*

> Most likely, the witches' sabbat was a fabrication of the witch-hunters, who seized upon admission of attendance at a gathering, meeting or feast, and twisted it into a diabolical affair. Victims who made such confessions were pressed to name others who had attended sabbats. In this manner, sometimes entire villages became implicated in Devil-worship.

Many other writers and historians also insist the sabbats never took place. Chances are the accused made the confessions to end their torture. It is very likely that many simply nodded yes to questions filled with lurid details of the demonic sabbat.

Author Rhoda Blumberg, in *Devils and Demons*, says, "There is not the slightest proof that sabbats ever took place. Descriptions of sabbat celebrations came from confessions of frightened, deranged, and tortured people." Other historians and writers note that accounts of the sabbat were prominent only in countries where the Inquisition was conducted and where torture was the most severe. The sabbat never gained much attention in witch trials in England or America.

Margaret A. Murray was an anthropologist writing in the 1920s and 1930s. (An anthropologist is a person who studies the customs and beliefs of

"There were usually several tables with three or four sorts of food, some very fine indeed."

Author Martin del Rio, *Disquisitionum Magicorum Libri Sex*, 1599

"The meat, whether perceived by the eyes or by the sense of smell, produces nausea. The taste of the food itself is so unpleasant and tart and bitter that it has to be vomited out as soon as tasted."

Author Nicholas Remy, *Demonolotry*, 1595

groups of people.) She maintained that sabbats did occur. But she viewed them as celebrations of a pagan religion that still existed in Europe even during the late Middle Ages and Renaissance. Sabbats, according to Murray, were held quarterly—on the second of February, the Eve of May (April 30), August first, and the Eve of November (October 31). These dates related to the cycles of nature, such as the changes of season and animal mating.

Many historians disagree with Murray that witches during the Inquisition were still practicing an organized pagan religion. However, they agree that in the ancient past, pagan festivals had been held at these times to celebrate the changing seasons and the increasing or waning power of the sun.

Greek and Roman Myths

According to historian Jeffrey B. Russell, in his book *A History of Witchcraft*, the church's portrayal of the wild sabbat activities was based, in part, on various Roman or Greek myths. For example, according to myth, followers of Dionysus, the Greek god of wine and merriment, used to meet at night. Their processions of mostly women were led by a priest and a goat, the symbol of the horned Dionysus. The celebrations included drinking, dancing, orgies, and ritual sacrifice of an animal.

According to another myth, the Roman goddess Diana, goddess of the moon and the hunt, led diabolical processions of witches. The tenth-century *Canon Episcopi* stated:

> It is not to be omitted that some wicked women, perverted by the Devil . . . believe and profess themselves, in the course of the night, to ride upon certain beasts with Diana, the goddess of the pagans, and an innumerable multitude of women, and in the silence of the dead of night to traverse great spaces of earth, and to obey her commands . . . and to be summoned to her service on certain nights.

Dianic cults still existed during the early Middle Ages (fifth and sixth centuries) and traces of those cults may have remained in the tenth century and later. According to Russell, the church may have blended the image of Diana with images of the Teutonic fertility goddess called Holda, Holle, or Holt to create the image of Diana as leader of witch processions. Holda was believed to lead the Wild Hunt, a procession of spirits and ghosts through the countryside. According to folktales, the Wild Hunters roamed the forests as child eaters and murderers. They were believed to be part human, part animal, and part spirit. People gradually transferred the image of these wild huntresses to witches who

Some historians believe that medieval people borrowed from Greek and Roman mythology in their depictions of sabbats. The Roman goddess Diana, for example, was said to lead diabolical processions of witches.

"All the coven did fly like cats, jackdaws, hares and rooks."

From a confession of Isobel Gowdie, 1662

"Who is there that is not led out of himself in dreams and nocturnal visions, and sees much when sleeping which he has never seen while awake?"

Canon Episcopi, tenth century

gathered at night to sacrifice and eat children and commit other monstrous acts.

Initiation

How did men and women become witches? Some accused witches testified they had been initiated as children—their mothers had taken them to sabbats and pledged them to service to their master, the devil. Adults, however, were introduced by members of the coven and decided of their own free will to become members.

New witches then underwent initiation at the sabbat. Accounts of initiation followed a common pattern. Witnesses testified that the devil was present at the rite as the initiate renounced the Christian faith. According to Pierre de Lancre, initiates declared, "I renounce and deny God, the blessed Virgin, the Saints, baptism, father, mother, relations, heaven, earth and all that is the world." Some men and women confessed to inquisitors that they also spit on the Christian cross. They then swore their loyalty to the devil, who gave them a new name and made a mark on them with his claw. He also assigned them a familiar and may have given them magic ointment. The new witch was required to kiss the devil's backside, witnesses said. This was a mockery of the act of kissing the pope's foot, a Christian tradition of personal humility and respect for the church. Sabbat ceremonies then began, with the new initiates having sex with the devil or his demons.

Initiation ceremonies might also include sacrifice of an animal or a child, according to some witches' confessions during the Inquisition. (The church had leveled that charge against many other heretical groups as well.)

The Coven

Another common belief was that witches belonged to covens, or small groups. Officials considered the coven a mockery of Christian congregations and practices. Cotton Mather, who was involved in the 1692 Salem witch-hunts, wrote in *On Witchcraft: Being the Wonders of the Invisible World*, "The witches do say that they form themselves much after the manner of the Congregational Churches, and that they have a Baptism, and a Supper [communion], and Officers among them, abominably resembling those of our Lord."

Margaret A. Murray maintained that covens were always made up of thirteen witches: "The number in a coven never varied, there were always thirteen, i.e., twelve members and the god." Murray also maintained that trial officials pressed for names in multiples of thirteen. But other historians say there is little evidence to uphold this theory. According to Rosemary Guiley, only eighteen trials included testimony that covens were made up of thirteen members.

Why thirteen, then? Thirteen has been thought an unlucky number since ancient times. It was also the number of people at the Last Supper—Jesus and his twelve apostles, one of whom betrayed him.

Witches were said to meet in small groups called covens. This illustration depicts the North Berwick coven in 1591. While some members drink in a cellar, one takes down the words of the devil, who is preaching from a pulpit. Outside, other witches boil a concoction in a cauldron meant to create a storm and sink a ship at sea.

Modern witch and author Laurie Cabot writes in *Power of the Witch*, "The association with Jesus was probably just another attempt by the Inquisition . . . to draw unfavorable analogies [comparisons] between Christianity and paganism by creating the myth that Witches pervert Christian customs." Cabot maintains that thirteen had nothing to do with Christianity but instead referred to the old lunar calendar with its thirteen full moons. She also adds, "Thirteen is just a good number of people in terms of simple group dynamics."

Murray used testimony from the European trials to conclude that each coven was ruled by a grandmaster who represented the Horned God. She said the church interpreted this Horned God to be the Christian devil, often portrayed as part man, part horned creature. But horned gods were part of many pagan traditions, dating back to the Stone Age, more than fifteen thousand years ago. In many cultures, he was the god of the underworld, animals, woodlands, and fertility. If the Horned God was actually present, the grandmaster became an officer at the sabbat rather than the leader. Each coven also had a summoner, often the grandmaster, who secretly called coven members to the next meeting. The summoner also kept the coven records and presented initiates. Murray also described the role of the coven maiden, whose rank was equal to that of the grandmaster but who had no executive power.

According to testimony in the North Berwick witches trial in Scotland in 1591, covens were independent but were also part of a regional network. But most historians doubt that covens even existed. They claim that, like so many other aspects of European witchcraft, the coven was largely invented by the Inquisition.

Similar Beliefs Around the World

If the claims about witches' practices are absurd, as many scholars claim, then why are so many of the features of European witchcraft also found in other cultures around the world?

Jeffrey Russell points out the many characteristics that European and African witches seemed to have in common: they were usually female and elderly, met at night assemblies, and left their bodies or assumed other shapes. They also rode brooms or other objects, flew naked through the air, and used magical ointments for various powers. Witches in both worlds also had familiars and performed circular dances. They were said to kill and eat children. "In all, at least fifty different motifs [themes] of European witchcraft can be found in other societies," Russell says. He writes:

> The worldwide similarity of sorcery beliefs constitutes the most curious and important dilemma in the study of witchcraft. When we find, centuries and continents apart, the idea of a night-hag seducing men and murdering children or a sorceress riding a broomstick, we are not entitled to dismiss the question of how these similarities arise.

Can it be explained by coincidence? Probably not—it seems almost impossible that there could be so many coincidences among so many distant cultures. One possibility is that humans share a mental structure that produces similar concepts, such as the wise man or woman, or the powerful old crone. That is, just because they are human, the people of many different cultures are likely to come up with similar beliefs. Psychologist Carl Jung said that humans share a "collective unconscious" that contains common dreams and images to which we all have access.

In any case, in Renaissance Europe, and later in America, these ideas about witches would bring about the deaths of hundreds of thousands of people, mostly women.

Witch stories exist all over the world, and share many similarities, including the kidnapping and eating of children.

Two

The Burning Times

Mercifully, the executioners had hung the condemned woman before tying her body to the stake to be consumed by fire. For only fire could completely wipe out the evil. But she had not been dead, only unconscious. She came to as the flames were devouring her body. Half-burned, screaming in agony, and begging for mercy, she dragged herself from the fire. But the crowd that had gathered for the public execution shoved her back into the flames. Death finally silenced her. Later, her family would receive a bill for the coal, wood, and sixteen loads of peat used to fuel the fire.

During the "burning times," between 1450 and 1700, hundreds of thousands of alleged witches, mostly women, were burned in a similar manner or hanged. To the authorities who made and enforced the laws many centuries ago, complete elimination of witchcraft was essential. If not, Satan and the forces of evil would prevail. Witches would continue to fly at night, eat babies, and destroy with their spells. People were not safe while witches lived.

The Inquisition

The burning times occurred during a period of the Inquisition. The Inquisition was a judicial institution started by the Roman Catholic Church in the

(Opposite page) A witch is burned at the stake in England. For over two centuries, hundreds of thousands of alleged witches were burned in this manner.

thirteenth century. It was most active in France, Germany, Italy, and Spain. Its purpose was to eliminate the church's enemies: non-Christians, such as Jews and Muslims, and Christian heretics, such as Cathars, Waldenses, and in the sixteenth century, Protestants. Christian teachings and law were also the foundation of most European governments, so heresy was a crime in most European countries.

The Inquisition was a brutal institution whose purpose was to punish people who opposed church teaching. Its aim was not justice, but confession and submission. Those brought before the inquisitors were tortured. If they refused to confess their heresy and convert to Catholicism, they could be executed.

Witchcraft was added to the church's list of heresies in 1320. But witches did not become a primary target of the Inquisition until after 1484. In that year, Pope Innocent VIII issued an edict that set off almost 250 years of torture and murder of accused witches. From then on, the authorities no longer waited for accusations of witchcraft to be brought to their attention; they actively searched for witches to prosecute.

According to historian Elliot Rose in his book *A*

Strange and unmarried women were not the only ones who were suspected of being witches. Here, two Dominican monks are burned by order of the Inquisition for allegedly signing pacts with the devil.

Razor for a Goat, the "storm-center" of witch-hunts was in the area where France, Germany, and Switzerland meet. Rose says that in Spain, the witch panic "seems to have left no trace at all." The Inquisition was not established in England. But England was also zealous in its pursuit and execution of alleged witches.

Some historians estimate that more than three hundred thousand people in Europe were executed as witches. More than one hundred thousand people were burned at the stake in Germany alone. Some witches today estimate that if those who died in prison were included in the count, the death toll would be millions.

The Church's Changing Stand Toward Witchcraft

Many Christians of the early Middle Ages, including priests, practiced pagan traditions and magic as well as Christianity. But as Christianity spread and became a stronger force, it sought to control the practice of magic. It made practice of harmful magic a civil crime. Beneficial magic, however, was not a crime—unless the results turned out to be harmful.

A succession of papal bulls (orders from the pope) gradually revised the church's position on witches and linked witchcraft with heresy. The writings of Thomas Aquinas (1226–1274), recognized as one of the church's greatest religious thinkers, had helped shift the church's stand on witchcraft. He had rejected the *Canon Episcopi* . He wrote that witches actually had sex with demons, could fly, and were capable of evil deeds. He believed that witches' ability to perform evil deeds implied that they had made a pact with the devil.

By the mid-fifteenth century, the church had completely rejected the *Canon Episcopi* stand that witchcraft was a foolish delusion. Witchcraft was no fantasy; it was a real evil that threatened humanity,

"Such a mass of evidence shows that till the end of the seventeenth century the Old Religion still counted large numbers of members."

Anthropologist Margaret A. Murray, *The God of the Witches*, 1931

"That this 'old religion' persisted secretly, without leaving any evidence, is of course possible, just as it is possible that below the surface of the moon lie extensive deposits of Stilton cheese. Anything is possible. But it is nonsense to assert the existence of something for which no evidence exists. The Murrayites ask us to swallow a most peculiar sandwich: a large piece of the wrong evidence between two thick slices of no evidence at all."

Historian Jeffrey B. Russell, *A History of Witchcraft*, 1980

Thomas Aquinas fed the witch hysteria by writing detailed accounts of the horrendous practices of witches.

the church declared. Not only did witches perform evil magic, they did so with the aid of the devil. The church was making the same accusations about witches that it had made about other heretics.

It was not until Pope Innocent VIII issued the Bull of 1484 that the all-out war against witchcraft began. Inquisitors Heinrich Kramer and Jakob Sprenger had approached Innocent VIII to intercede with local authorities. Kramer and Sprenger complained the authorities were impeding their efforts to try witches. Innocent issued the 1484 document. It stated that some men and women "gave themselves over to devils male and female, and by their incantations, charms and conjurings . . . ruin and cause to perish the offspring of women, the foal of animals, the products of the earth." The bull went on to detail the other results of witchcraft and instructed local officials to help Sprenger and Kramer to prosecute witches.

The Witches Hammer

Sprenger and Kramer included this bull in their book, the *Malleus Maleficarum*, published first in Germany only two years after the papal bull had been issued. *Malleus Maleficarum* is Latin for *The Witches Hammer*. The *Malleus Maleficarum* guided civil and church law for more than two centuries. Dozens of editions were distributed throughout Europe. It became the second best-selling book in Europe—next to the Bible.

Sprenger and Kramer's justification for witch-hunting, prosecution, and persecution was based on one short, out-of-context verse from the Bible: "Thou shall not suffer a witch to live" (Exodus 22:17). According to sixteenth-century writer Reginald Scot and later scholars, however, the Hebrew word that was translated as "witch" usually referred to diviners, astrologers, or poisoners—not witches. Sprenger and Kramer also supported their

MALLEVS MALEFICARVM,
MALEFICAS ET EARVM
hæresim frameâ conterens,

EX VARIIS AVCTORIBVS COMPILATVS,
& in quatuor Tomos iuftè diftributus,

QVORVM DVO PRIORES VANAS DÆMONVM
verfutias , praftigiofas eorum'delufiones , fuperftitiofas Strigimagarum
cæremonias , horrendos etiam cum illis congreffus ; exactam denique
tam peftifera fectæ difquifitionem , & punitionem complectuntur.
Tertius praxim Exorciftarum ad Dæmonum , & Strigimagarum male-
ficia de Chrifti fidelibus pellenda ; Quartus verò Artem Doctrinalem ,
Benedictionalem , & Exorcifmalem continent.

TOMVS PRIMVS.
Indices Auctorum , capitum , rerûmque non defunt.

Editio nouiffima , infinitis penè mendis expurgata ; cuique acceffit Fuga
Dæmonum & Complementum artis exorcifticæ.

Vir fiue mulier,in quibus Pythonicus, vel diuinationis fuerit fpiritus, morte moriatur
Leuitici cap. 10.

LVGDVNI,
Sumptibus CLAVDII BOVRGEAT,fub figno Mercurij Galli.

M. DC. LXIX.
CVM PRIVILEGIO REGIS.

The *Malleus Maleficarum* described the habits of witches in gruesome detail and gave instructions on how to identify, try, and destroy witches. It was a best-selling book in medieval Europe.

case for destruction of witchcraft with writings from Aristotle, Thomas Aquinas, and Saint Augustine.

The *Malleus Maleficarum* was divided into three major sections. The first part declares that the devil and his helpers—witches, sorcerers, and other demons—did their evil deeds with the permission of God. Such a claim was necessary if people were to see the Christian God as an all-powerful being and greater than Satan. If the devil acted without God's permission, the devil would be as powerful as God.

The next section of the book deals with how witches cast spells and bewitch people and animals. It includes gruesome tales of children being abducted and sacrificed and of sexual acts between the devil and witches. These lurid details were taken from testimony of accused witches during trials conducted by Kramer and Sprenger.

The book's final section describes the legal procedures for trying witches. It includes recommendations on how to obtain testimony, inflict torture, and pass sentence. In most cases, execution was the proper punishment, the authors said. They also reassured officials who might have felt a twinge of guilt about the executions: God would not allow the conviction and execution of innocent people.

The Witches of Arras

The trial of the witches of Arras, France, was one of the earliest mass witch-hunts. It occurred from 1459 to 1460, even before the *Malleus Maleficarum* was published, so the officials did not have the benefit of its guidance. But they did know that heretics worshiped the devil and that all witches were heretics.

The events opened with the arrest of a hermit, possibly a member of the Waldenses, a small, early Protestant group that had broken away from the church. According to the church, the Waldenses, like witches, worshiped the devil and held wild celebrations in his honor. Under torture, the hermit admitted that one night he had attended a celebration at which the devil was present. The hermit named other people who had been present, including a prostitute and an elderly poet. The hermit was burned at the stake, and the two he named were arrested. They, in turn, accused still others.

The judges and inquisitors drew forth confession after confession of guilt. Brutal torture was enough to make most people admit to just about any crime. Others confessed because officials promised lighter sentences if they confessed and named other guilty parties.

Although many of the victims of the witch-hunts were poor, in Arras even wealthy and important people were accused, including church bishops and cardinals. Inquisitors were convinced that witchcraft had taken a firm hold on the region. People who protested the torture and executions were also condemned.

The Arras witch-hunt died down only after news of the events scared off foreign merchants. Since Arras was a center of commerce and manufacturing, the loss of trade made people take notice.

The arrests finally stopped at the end of 1460 when the duke of Burgundy intervened. The next year, the Parliament and the bishop of Arras, who had been absent during the trials, ordered the release of all prisoners accused of witchcraft. Thirty years later, the Parliament condemned the actions of the officials who had ordered the cruel tortures and executions.

But despite the authorities' displeasure with the events at Arras, this was just the beginning of the torture and killings of supposed witches in France and much of Europe.

Brutal Torture in Germany

Bamberg and Wurzburg, small states in Germany, were the sites of some of the most brutal treatment. In Bamberg, the ruling prince-bishop established a witch-prosecution machine, with full-time lawyers, torturers, and executioners. He even built a special witch prison with well-equipped torture chambers. In Wurzburg, the ruling prince-bishop tortured and executed nine hundred alleged witches, including more than three hundred children between the ages of three and four. These two ruling prince-bishops

"It is hard to satisfy modern writers on witchcraft, who insist on censuring the sixteenth and seventeenth century on a basis of modern rationalism. It is quite certain that if some of those who now sit in judgment on the witch-prosecutors had been witch judges, no defendant would ever have escaped."

Historian George Lyman Kittredge, *Witchcraft in Old and New England,* 1929

"Justice was perverted and thousands of innocent men and women died on the false evidence of envious or vengeful accusers."

Author Ronald Seth, *Witches and Their Craft,* 1967

In Bamberg, Germany, the torture and trial of witches became a science. These are a few of the methods of torture used in Bamberg to elicit confessions.

also happened to be cousins.

Informers turned in their fellow citizens on the slightest suspicion: a cross word or curse, an argument with a neighbor, an angry look. If a hailstorm destroyed crops or a child got sick, witchcraft was said to be the cause, and someone had to be held responsible. Victims were denied legal counsel. But no one would dare defend them anyway!

The accused were stripped, shaved, and examined for witch's marks or devil's marks. Some confessions were "voluntary." That is, the accused confessed after the examination or after "light" torture, such as whipping, or after merely hearing what the torturer had planned for them. Most of the accused, however, required more severe methods.

The torture that took place in Bamberg and other German states, as well as in France, Italy, Switzerland, and Scotland, was appalling in its brutality. It should be noted that torture was not limited to alleged witches. Heretics and criminals of many types suffered torture as well. By the time of the witch-hunts, torture had become an acceptable means of extracting confessions. The authorities had become masters at inflicting pain and taking the accused just to the edge of death. Defendants were stretched on the rack; they were burned with red-hot irons, sometimes internally; their bones were smashed; their thumbs and toes were crushed with thumbscrews. Other atrocities are too vile to describe. Accused witches were forced to confess to attending sabbats, poisoning people, dishonoring Catholic rituals, having sex with Satan and demons, or practicing magic with Satan's aid. Anyone who interfered was also brutalized and burned at the stake.

Under torture, most accused could be induced to confess to anything. Many made up stories simply to stop the pain. Some confessed quickly when they were forced to watch their families being tortured. Local rulers profited by seizing the property of defendants.

Protection from Witches

A prisoner who refused to confess, even under torture, was obviously protected by the devil, authorities contended. Meanwhile, court officials and torturers protected themselves from bewitchment by spraying their equipment with holy water, wearing amulets (charms), and constantly crossing themselves with the Christian sign of the cross. In effect, they were practicing magic, the very crime for which they were torturing and

"It would be interesting to know how many of the hundreds of thousands of men and women who now suffered had any real interest in witchcraft, let alone engaged in even the most innocent recital of traditional spells or charms. But the witch-finders had no difficulty in finding people to burn, arresting them on the slightest suspicion, often because some neighbor spoke ill of them."

Authors Derek and Julia Parker, *The Power of Magic*, 1992

"It has never yet been known that an innocent person has been punished on suspicion of witchcraft, and there is no doubt that God will never permit such a thing to happen."

Inquisitors Jakob Sprenger and Heinrich Kramer, *Malleus Maleficarum*, 1486

In this illustration from a newsletter published in 1555, three witches are publicly burned in Denneburg.

killing others!

Accused witch Johannes Junius, mayor of Bamberg, wrote to his daughter from prison. He endured agony from the thumbscrews and the strappado, one of the most horrendous tortures. After describing the torture, he wrote:

> When at last the executioner led me back into the prison he said to me: "Sir, I beg you, for God's sake confess something, whether it be true or not. Invent something, for you cannot endure the torture which you will be put to; and even if you bear it all, yet you will not escape, not even if you were an earl, but one torture will follow another until you say you are a witch."

Ferdinand II, the Holy Roman emperor, issued a decree opposing the brutality practiced in Bamberg and Wurzburg. But the persecution ended only when the ruling prince-bishops died in the early 1630s.

Witchcraft in England

England was also responsible for its share of horrors against alleged witches. But the Inquisition was not established in England, and witchcraft was not a crime of heresy there. Instead, witchcraft remained closely associated with sorcery, such as keeping familiars and performing evil magic that caused harm to people and livestock. However, the authorities did believe the devil helped witches perform these evil deeds.

The Parliament passed its first statute against witchcraft in 1542. It was revoked five years later but replaced with a new law in 1563. The new law imposed the death penalty for murder by witchcraft or invoking evil spirits even if no harm came from it. Punishment was less severe for other uses of magic.

Chelmsford, in Essex, was the location of four important trials during the sixteenth and seventeenth centuries. The first trial occurred in 1566 and was the first major trial under the new law. Three women—Elizabeth Francis, Agnes Waterhouse, and Joan Waterhouse, Agnes's daughter—were charged under the Act of 1563.

Francis, charged with bewitching a baby, confessed to the crime of witchcraft. She admitted that

Although the Inquisition was never established in England, witches were still vigorously hunted and hanged, tortured, and burned at the stake.

she had been taught witchcraft by her grandmother who gave her a familiar, a white-spotted cat named Sathan. She testified that Sathan brought her wealth. She also said Sathan helped her get her revenge against a man who refused to marry her—the familiar saw to it that the man lost all of his wealth and then killed him. Sathan also performed other evil deeds at Francis's bidding, including killing Francis's own child. The accused woman stated that each time Sathan did something for her, the cat required a drop of her blood.

Francis said she grew tired of Sathan after fifteen years and traded him to Agnes Waterhouse. Waterhouse confessed at her trial that Sathan helped her bewitch a man who soon died. She also said she sent Sathan to kill another man and to destroy her neighbors' livestock, geese, and property. She denied feeding Sathan her blood, but officials found a supposed witch's mark on her.

Waterhouse also testified that her eighteen-year-old daughter had sent Sathan in the form of a black dog to bewitch a twelve-year-old neighbor.

Elizabeth Francis was sentenced to a year in prison, and Joan Waterhouse was found not guilty. Agnes Waterhouse was hung.

In 1579, four women were charged with bewitchment. Three were hanged, including repeat offender Elizabeth Francis. In 1589, nine women and one man were charged and tried; most of the testimony came from children. Testimony about familiars figured largely in the trial. Four of the defendants were hanged; three were found not guilty. The fates of the others are unknown.

King James's Law

King James I introduced a new law against witchcraft in 1604. It outlawed pacts with the devil and devil worship, the most prominent features of witchcraft in the rest of Europe. During the next few decades, the themes of the witches' sabbat and pacts with the devil appeared in English witch trials.

The witch-hunts in England peaked in the 1640s. The bloodiest witch-hunt in Chelmsford took place during this time. The notorious witch-hunter Matthew Hopkins claimed credit for bringing at least thirty-eight people to trial there. Twenty-nine were condemned, according to Hopkins.

Matthew Hopkins, like others in England, made a very decent living from hunting witches. Chelmsford was only one of his many "successes." He is believed to have brought about the executions of at

An illustration depicts Matthew Hopkins, renowned witch-hunter, with imps and familiars of witches. Hopkins made a decent living from his trade, and he may have been directly responsible for the deaths of over two hundred alleged witches.

least 230 witches.

Hopkins, like other witch-hunters, was paid for convictions, not accusations. Although torture was illegal, Hopkins was a master of using it to secure confessions. Torture in England, for the most part, was not as brutal as in other parts of Europe. Starvation and sleep deprivation were effective enough. But Hopkins also walked defendants relentlessly in their cells until their feet became blistered and infected. After wearing his victims down, he secured nods and one-word answers that sufficed as confessions.

Hopkins also used the swim test: defendants were bound, then thrown in the water. If they floated, they surely were witches, because even the water rejected them. If they sank, they were not guilty. Unfortunately, many innocent defendants drowned when officials could not rescue them in time.

Skin pricking was also a favorite tactic of Hopkins and other witch-hunters. This involved sticking a needle into the skin to find spots that were not sensitive to pain. These places were sup-

A favorite torture used to discover witches was the water trial, which was also impossible to survive. If a person floated, he or she was a witch; if he or she sank (and inevitably drowned), the individual was pronounced innocent.

posedly witch's marks. Hopkins is said to have resorted to trickery to be sure he would find witches and thus stay in business. He was said to have used retractable needles so that he would be sure to find "nonsensitive" spots.

The Opposition

Even though criticism could mean imprisonment or death, a few brave souls in Europe and in England not only opposed the witch-hunts, they actually wrote books protesting them.

Johann Weyer, a Belgian doctor, published a book in 1563 in which he maintained that the devil himself stirred up the fear of witchcraft. He accused the church of playing right into the devil's hands. Weyer did not dispute that a devil existed. In fact, he claimed that more than seven million devils and demons existed and were organized into divisions of 6,666 each. He did not dispute that some witches made pacts with the devil. But the witches did not perform evil, Satan did, he said. He claimed that most witches were outcasts and mentally ill women. They could not harm anyone, and they certainly did not employ supernatural methods, according to Weyer. And if the accused were not capable of magic, did they really deserve to be killed? The doctor escaped punishment for his strong stand against the witch-hunts, largely because he was protected by his powerful patient, the duke of Julich.

In 1584, *The Discoverie of Witchcraft* by Reginald Scot was published in England. Scot's writings represented the prevailing superstitions of the day, superstitions that he mostly disproved. Scot condemned people who attributed supernatural power to witches. He wrote that such powers belonged only to God and that anyone who thought a witch could have divine powers was "a blasphemer, an idolater, and full of gross impiety."

"Those too who let the witches escape, or who do not punish them with the utmost rigor, may rest assured that they will be abandoned by God to the mercy of the witches. And the country which shall tolerate this will be scourged with pestilences, famines, and wars; and those which shall take vengeance on the witches will be blessed by him and will make his anger cease."

Demonologist Jean Bodin, *Demonomanie des Sorciers*, 1580

"He that attributeth to a witch, such divine powers, as duly and only appertaineth unto God . . . is in heart a blasphemer, an idolator, and full of gross impiety, although he neither go nor send to her for assistance."

Author Reginald Scot, *The Discoverie of Witchcraft*, 1584

An illustration from Reginald Scot's 1584 volume *The Discoverie of Witchcraft* depicts a formal magical circle for the invocation of demons. Scot described witchcraft in order to disprove it.

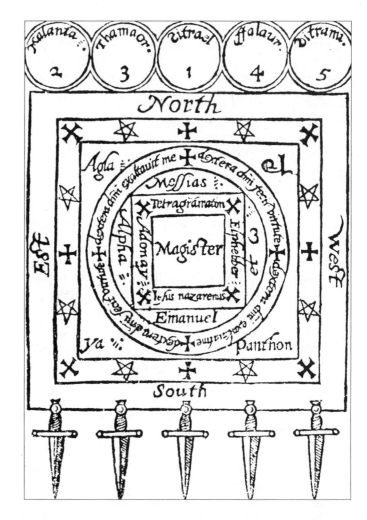

Weyer and Scot questioned whether any of the accused were actually practicing magic or worshipping the devil. That debate has continued.

Did Witches Worship the Devil?

Most modern historians maintain that the people executed as witches were innocent victims. A small minority of the accused may have been devil worshippers, they say. But for most alleged witches, their only crimes were clinging to their folk traditions, or being women, healers, folk magicians, mentally ill people, social outcasts, or political enemies of the church or government.

But if the witches did not really worship the devil or even practice evil sorcery, then what were the witch-hunts really about? During a period of great religious, social, and political upheaval, the people, the church, and the governments needed scapegoats, historians say. The victims were merely unfortunate people, caught up in the hysteria of the time.

A War Against Women

Misogyny (hatred and fear of women) was one leading cause of the witch-hunts, say some historians and contemporary witches.

Witch Laurie Cabot writes that when Christianity became the official religion of the Roman Empire in the fourth century, "Woman fell from being a natural reflection of the Great Goddess and Mother of All Living Things to the lowly position of a slave, not made in the image of God, and possibly not having a soul."

Cabot says that by the late Middle Ages, the word "witch" meant "woman,"

> especially any woman who criticized the patriarchal policies of the Christian church. . . . Church literature grew increasingly strident [harsh and insistent] in its teaching that women were a threat to the community because they knew magic. Over the years the campaign worked: In the popular mind women who knew the ways of the Craft were considered evil.

King James of England and Scotland, writing at the beginning of the seventeenth century, said that for every twenty-one witches, twenty were women. Historian and writer Selma R. Williams says that this accusation is not surprising. Men considered women otherworldly because women could bring forth new life from their bodies. She writes in *Riding the Nightmare* that women were also "the earthly personification of Mother Nature," so they

"We instinctively understand that during the long centuries when women were the semislaves of society, they were naturally drawn to witchcraft as a cure for their powerlessness, a means of manipulating a world that otherwise painfully manipulated them."

Erica Jong, *Witches*, 1981

"What can be the cause that there are twenty women given to that craft where there is one man?
Answer: The reason is easy, for as that sex is frailer than man is, so it is easier to be entrapped in these gross snares of the Devil's . . . Where the Devil finds greatest ignorance and barbarity . . . there assails he the grossest."

King James of England and Scotland, *Daemonologie*, 1597

were blamed for storms, droughts, floods, and extreme temperatures.

The late Middle Ages and the Renaissance had been ravaged by plague and war. New industry was bringing about financial and social change. The infant death rate was very high. People were scared, Williams says, and they believed that a sinister force was at work. Jews had been convenient scapegoats for several hundred years, but gradually witches—mostly women—began sharing the blame. Both Jews and witches were believed to kill and eat babies. That would explain why infant after infant was dying. By the 1500s, however, witches were becoming the primary scapegoats, since most Jews had fled to eastern Europe.

Men also feared and blamed the midwives who attended to mother and infant at delivery. According to Williams, men believed that women attended witches' sabbats to learn about pregnancy and childbirth. The devil, of course, was in attendance. Men accused the midwife of using diabolical witchcraft if anything went wrong during childbirth.

Three witches with their familiars, seventeenth century. Some scholars believe that the entire witch craze was an expression of misogyny. Women, especially independent women, were scapegoated.

Miscarriages, stillbirths, and problems for the mother were common, so midwives were easy targets of witch hysteria. Even if mother and child were healthy, the midwife was still suspected of using magic to help them through the dangers and mystery of childbirth.

Contemporary historian Jeffrey Russell says the hatred of women also was due to demographics (the way the population is distributed)—the growing number of women living alone. Men were killed in war or at sea, leaving wives, sisters, mothers, or daughters without a man at home. Women were marrying later—or not at all. The number of women in convents was declining. And then, as now, women tended to live longer than men. Many men thought women lived longer because of magic.

Easy Targets of Blame

Women living without the protection or authority of men had no rights or power. They were easy targets of blame when things went wrong. And magic was one of the ways women made things go wrong, the reasoning of the day went. Women may very well have resorted to magic, but they did so because it was one of the few alternatives available to them, Russell explains. The "evil eye," a curse, muttering, or loitering were all seen as spellcasting.

Russell says the church played a big role in the misogyny. But if witches—mostly women—were labeled as magicians or heretics, maybe it was because they were, he says. Because they were so powerless in medieval society, they may very well have turned to the heretical sects that allowed women more rights. He also blames other traditions for the misogyny of Europe and later of colonial America. Judaism, and then Christianity, had eliminated the idea of the goddess and had made the supreme deity a male. Both also had cast

An illustration from 1537 depicts an old maid as a witch. Scholars believe that the number of women living alone, vulnerable and powerless, threatened the prescribed social order and made easy targets for vindictive neighbors.

women in the role of evildoer in the cosmic struggle between good and evil, starting with Eve in the Garden of Eden.

The Clash of Religions

According to some writers, witch-hunts were an expression of the clash of religions. They say the burning times were the result of a chain of events probably set in motion a thousand years before the witch-hunts hit their peak.

The witch-hunts were the front lines of a battle between the Catholic Church and paganism, some historians say. But the battle between the Catholic Church and paganism was not the religious conflict that contributed to the witch-hunts. For no sooner had the church finally established itself as the state religion, than the Protestant Reformation crept in. This sixteenth-century movement threatened the church's newfound supremacy. Witches became a pawn in the power struggle between the Protestant and Catholic churches. Each accused the other's followers of being witches. Even though Protestants were themselves targets of the Catholic Inquisition, they were certainly not allies of the accused witches. Martin Luther, a Reformation leader, declared, "I would have no pity on these witches. I would burn them all." Cabot writes in *Power of the Witch:*

> The history of Christianity is the history of persecution. Christian forces have consistently harassed, persecuted, tortured and put to death people whose spirituality differed from their own—Pagans, Jews, Muslims. . . . Christian armies and clergy . . . have repeatedly failed to see the sacred wisdom in other cultural traditions based on different perceptions of the divine power.

It is difficult not to point an accusing finger at Christianity. But Christianity alone was not to blame.

Other Social Conditions

Other factors also were operating to trigger the witch-hunts, according to a contemporary witch, Starhawk. Increasing commercialism meant that land was considered a possession. Pagan, earth-centered culture held that no one owned the land; it belonged to the community. But now property owners were fencing off their lands and displacing peasants. The time was unsettled, and unsettled times called for scapegoats. The church and the wealthy launched witch-hunts against those who held to the old ways and who fought for the old pagan view of land.

The medical profession was also gaining power. Witches and other healers were a threat to the university-trained doctors. The *Malleus Maleficarum* said, "If a woman dare to cure without having studied, she is a Witch and must die."

Healers and midwives were seen as witches because they used herbs and magic and other remedies. Many of their remedies were more effective and much less painful than the medical profession's cures, such as bleeding and using leeches. These healing women could provide digestive aids, contraceptives, pain relievers, and other remedies. Surprisingly, many people of the time considered their healing powers subversive because they could relieve pain! People were supposed to suffer, especially during childbirth; that was part of God's plan, the church said. If these women were able to ease the pain of childbirth, surely this was wrong—evil and satanic.

Most historians question the existence of organized devil-worshipping cults in Europe during the Burning Times. But another school of thought claims that cults did exist. However, these cults were not worshipping the devil, but rather ancient pagan gods.

The theory had been around since the late 1800s. But anthropologist Margaret Murray, writing in the 1920s and 1930s, helped to give it validity. According to Murray, victims of witch-hunts were actually practicing an ancient fertility religion dating back to the Stone Age. They were worshipping a male Horned God, Dianus. The stories of devil worship, she said, derived from the worship of the Horned God. Stories of sex with the devil probably came from the fertility rites of the ancient religion, in which members had sex with the Horned God or his human representative in order to ensure abundance across the land.

Confusion About Pagan Beliefs

Historians have dismissed Murray's theory. They have argued that the pagan cult she described never actually existed. They agree that many charges against witches may have been based on confusion about pagan beliefs. They also recognize that the church had incorporated pagan holidays and magic into its own practice. But only remnants of pagan belief remained after Christianity spread, they said, and Murray's witch cult was a composite of pagan practices. It was not the survival of a full-fledged religion as Murray said.

But witch Sybil Leek thinks otherwise. She agrees with Murray's version of history and writes:

> At the time of the Inquisition the Old Religion had millions of followers and even allowing for many of the deaths having been caused by personal enmity, the records of

A witch is seduced by the devil.

witches persecuted in Europe must make us realize that this was no tiny secret society. Europe was not so highly populated then as today, but the proportion of witches to those of other religions was about one to one.

The Persecutions End

Whatever the reasons or basis for the witch-hunts, they finally came to an end in Europe and in England by the close of the seventeenth century. The legal and religious machinery that had set the witch-hunts in motion had finally wound down.

Officials seemed to have become alarmed at the large number of people being accused and executed. They had to consider what the witch-hunts meant. Were they in a losing battle with the devil? Or, if God still ruled, were the persecutions a mistake?

The practice of folk magic survived the witch-hunts and continues today. But belief in diabolical witchcraft has slowly disappeared. It flared up in Puritan New England, especially in Salem in 1692. But generally across Europe, it had been on the decline during the latter half of the seventeenth century. A view of a more rational and ordered universe was taking hold. People became more likely to blame illness or disasters on natural causes rather than on magic or the devil.

Prosecution of witches ended in most countries by the middle of the eighteenth century. By the late eighteenth century, most people wondered how anyone could ever have believed in witches!

Three

The Salem Witch-Hunts: Why?

One of the last episodes of witch hysteria in the Western world took place in Salem, Massachusetts, in 1692. The Salem witch-hunt was the largest witch-hunt in colonial New England. Between 1620 and 1725, about 350 people (almost 80 percent of them women) were accused of witchcraft in New England; 185 of those cases happened in one year in Salem. Of the thirty-five executions for witchcraft in all of colonial New England, nineteen took place during the Salem witch-hunts; fourteen of the victims were women.

The Hysteria Begins

The name *Salem* was taken from the Hebrew word *shalom* meaning "peace." However, Salem, Massachusetts, founded in 1626, was not the peaceful community its name promised. Two Salems existed—Salem Village and Salem Town—and political and social tensions ran high between them. Salem Town had legal and religious authority over Salem Village (now Danvers, Massachusetts). Many villagers wanted their community to separate from the town. Samuel Parris, who became the village's minister in 1689, was a controversial member of the community from the time he arrived. He quickly became a leading speaker for village independence.

(Opposite page) A scene from the Salem witch trials shows one of the girls pointing an accusing finger at a "witch." The trials were a study in group hysteria.

The village separated into pro-Parris and anti-Parris forces. Members of the very powerful Putnam family were Parris's leading allies and defenders.

Parris became one of the loudest voices calling for condemnation of accused witches. Ironically, the outbreak of accusations began in his own home and quickly spread to the home of his allies, Thomas and Ann Putnam. Some historians have accused these two families of being among the chief instigators of the witch-hunts.

The Girls Become Afflicted

Reverend and Mrs. Parris owned two slaves—Tituba and John Indian. Parris had brought the slave couple from Barbados, where he had served as a merchant before becoming a minister. The Parrises had a nine-year-old daughter, Betty; the Parrises' niece, eleven-year-old Abigail Williams, also lived in the household.

During the long New England winter, Tituba probably entertained Betty and Abigail with stories of her native Barbados and the practice of voodoo and magic. Fascinated with the forbidden topic of the occult, the girls probably shared their new knowledge with their friends. Betty, Abigail, Ann Putnam Jr., and others began dabbling with fortune-telling. They made a primitive "crystal ball" as Betty and Abigail had seen Tituba do—by floating an egg white in a glass of water. But when one of the girls thought she saw in the glass the image of a coffin—signifying death—the girls apparently became scared.

Betty and the other girls began having fits in January. Reverend John Hale witnessed the fits. Years later, he included this description in *A Modest Inquiry into the Nature of Witchcraft*, his soul-searching account of the events at Salem: "Their arms, necks and backs were turned this way and that way, and returned back again, so as it was

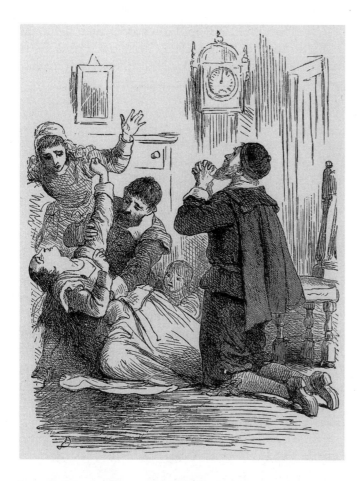

A girl possessed by witchcraft is delivered from her torment with prayer.

impossible for them to do of themselves, and beyond the power of any epileptic fits, or natural disease to effect."

Other symptoms included loss of hearing, speech, and sight; loss of memory; loss of appetite; hallucinations; and sensations of being pinched by invisible hands and bitten by invisible mouths. They even had marks on their skin as if they had been pinched or bitten. The girls also made barking, braying, and choking sounds. On occasion, they would run around on the floor on all fours. Sometimes they went into convulsions; sometimes, they became absolutely motionless and simply stared.

Doctors could not find a medical reason for the girls' strange behavior. They concluded that Betty and the other girls, who ranged in age from nine to twenty, were bewitched.

Tituba's Witch Cake

Mary Sibley, the aunt of one of the afflicted girls, called on Tituba with a plan to use magic to unmask the witches. She asked Tituba to make a witch cake out of rye and the girls' urine. (Urine was believed to have occult power and was a common ingredient in the casting of spells.) The cake was then fed to the Parrises' dog, who Sibley suspected was a familiar. Sibley believed that if the girls were truly bewitched, either the dog would become afflicted, too, or it would identify the witch.

Sibley's actions angered Parris. He accused her of "going to the Devil for help against the Devil." He preached at her from the pulpit: "The Devil hath been raised among us, and his rage is vehement and terrible, and when he shall be silenced, the Lord only knows."

Tituba no doubt told the young girls of Salem about voodoo and witchcraft in her native land, Barbados. She probably had little idea, though, that her entertaining tales would result in destruction of life.

But some people thought the witch cake had worked. For when pressed for answers as to who had bewitched them, the girls started naming Salem citizens.

Although Mary Sibley had resorted to witchcraft to seek out the witches, she was not accused of any crime. As the craze went on, it became obvious that the authorities were selective. They dismissed some charges as absurd. They seemed to pursue most strongly people with little power or people against whom Parris or the Putnams already had a gripe.

The Accusations Begin

One of the first accusations was leveled against Tituba. The girls also implicated Sarah Good and Sarah Osborne. On February 29, 1692, authorities issued warrants for these women's arrests. That these three women were accused of witchcraft is not surprising to most historians. Each was considered "different" or an "outcast" in the community. Tituba was a black slave, a mysterious woman from a mysterious land, with a religion and traditions that were very different from those of the repressed Puritans. Neither she nor the two Sarahs attended church, an offense against God, church, and community.

Sarah Good was a beggar, feeding herself and her daughter on handouts. Rather than feeling sorry for her, other citizens believed that if she had to beg it must be because God was punishing her for some sin. She also stirred resentment because of her reported mean-spiritedness: she grumbled even when people did give her handouts. Her independence and impolite manner were unacceptable behavior for a woman. And to top it all off, she smoked a pipe.

Sarah Osborne was ill and bedridden. She had offended her neighbors years earlier by marrying her indentured servant and perhaps even living

The girls accused Tituba of witchcraft first. Typical of those accused of being witches, Tituba, a black, mysterious woman, was an easy mark.

A scene from the Salem witch trials shows one of the girls falling down in convulsions at the trial of an alleged witch. Almost all of those accused by the girls had something in common—offending the local gentry or being alone and powerless.

with him before the marriage. She had also incurred the wrath of her first husband's relatives, the Putnams, when she contested her husband's will.

When the three accused women appeared before the town magistrates, the afflicted girls began twitching and falling into convulsions. The girls claimed that the accused women's "specters" or spirits were tormenting them by pinching and biting them or by appearing as birds or animals. None but the afflicted could see the specters, but spectral evidence was as damning as any physical evidence.

Osborne denied she had bewitched the children. But if she had not, why did they fall into fits at the sight of her, the court asked. Osborne suggested that perhaps the devil could impersonate an innocent person.

Tituba confessed to being a witch. Perhaps she was afraid not to, since Parris had beaten and threatened her. She also accused Sarah Good and Sarah Osborne of being witches. The three women were put in prison to await trial. No trials could be held yet because Massachusetts had lost its royal charter, which had granted it legal status as an English colony with the right to govern itself. Without a charter, the colony had no authority to try capital cases.

The accusations continued through the spring of 1692. The number of afflicted was increasing, as even some adults began claiming to be tormented by unseen specters. The next round of accusations was leveled against two well-respected churchwomen. Martha Corey was a strong and outspoken woman, but she was vulnerable to accusation because she stood to inherit land when her elderly husband died. She had also been skeptical of the budding witch-craft hysteria. The elderly Rebecca Nurse was a member of a family that had been feuding with the Putnams.

Dorcas Good, the daughter of Sarah Good, was among those jailed to await trial. The afflicted girls claimed Dorcas had learned evil witchcraft from her mother. Special chains had to be made to hold her in her cell because the regular chains were too large for her small limbs—she was only five years old.

Officials came to believe that the devil had invaded the entire region. They took the girls to nearby communities to flush out witches. Before the witch-hunt was over, people from more than twenty other communities had been accused.

At the end of April, Reverend George Burroughs of Wells, Maine, was arrested. Burroughs had been the minister at Salem Village. He had left largely because of disagreements with the Putnam family. The girls accused Burroughs of being the head of the coven and the mastermind behind the entire witchcraft outbreak.

The Trials Begin

In May, the new royal governor, Sir William Phips, arrived in New England with the new charter. He established a special Court of Oyer and Terminer (a court to hear [oyer] and to determine [terminer]) to try the accused witches of Salem and nearby towns.

"The hysteria of the inner circle of afflicted girls was generally well controlled. With remarkable precision, they could turn their outbursts on and off at will. These bewitched young girls were able to charm their audiences. One might say they were more bewitching than bewitched."

Historian Enders A. Robinson, *The Devil Discovered*, 1991

"One is not obliged to accept the verdict of the popular historians that the children were deceitful, wicked, malicious and dishonest. History has been unkind to them long enough. They were not impostors or pests or frauds; they were not cold-blooded malignant brats. They were sick children in the worst sort of mental distress—living in fear for their very lives and the welfare of their immortal souls."

Physician and amateur historian Ernest Caulfield, *American Journal of Diseases of Children*, May 1943

Bridget Bishop was the first prisoner tried and condemned by the court. She was hanged on June 8 at a place that became known as "Witches Hill" or "Gallows Hill" on the western side of town. She was buried in a shallow grave there, since a proper Christian burial was not allowed.

Five more executions took place on July 19, including that of Sarah Good. As Good stood on the scaffold awaiting hanging, Reverend Noyes urged her to confess. She answered, "I am no more a witch than you are a wizard, and if you take away my life, God will give you blood to drink." Was it coincidence—or witchcraft—that in 1717 he died choking on his own blood? Sarah Osborne had died in prison before she came to trial. Tituba's life was spared because she had confessed, but she remained in prison after her trial. Eventually she was sold to pay for her prison costs.

Evidence against the accused witches had consisted almost entirely of the afflicted girls' claims that unseen specters were tormenting them. But reliance on this evidence began to bother some members of the court. They wrestled with the

Martha Corey is tried for witchcraft. Her true "crimes" seem to be that she was a strong, outspoken woman who doubted the girls' evidence.

Accused "witches" are led to Gallows Hill to be hung. Eventually, the girls would go beyond their own town, accusing others of witchcraft.

question Rebecca Nurse had raised in her own defense: Was it possible for the devil to take the shape of an innocent person in order to afflict the girls?

The court asked the clergy to rule on this question. The Reverend Cotton Mather and his father, the Reverend Increase Mather, warned the judges against placing too much emphasis on spectral evidence. They cautioned the judges to look at other evidence: Did the afflicted collapse at the sight of the accused? Was the afflicted released from her twitching and torments at a touch from the accused? A "yes" to either question was proof of guilt.

The court pressed for confessions or concrete evidence similar to that used in European trials. Had anyone seen the accused fly? Did the accused show any supernatural abilities, such as superior strength or mind reading? Did the accused have a "witch's tit" from which a familiar might feed?

The court also looked for direct cause-and-effect evidence that the accused had actually bewitched someone. For example, at the same moment that John Putnam was accusing Rebecca Nurse of witchcraft, his eight-week-old baby began having fits; it died two days later. Obviously, the court reasoned, the baby's death was Nurse's revenge.

Other evidence included the accused's inability to recite the Lord's Prayer properly, since, according to popular belief, witches recited the prayer backwards at their sabbats. However, last-minute ability to recite the prayer did not necessarily spare the lives of the condemned. Five witches were

Although the persons involved at the Salem witch trials attempted to make them scientific and like the courts in England, they must have seemed almost farcical. The girls would have been convulsing on the floor, the crowds who came to attend would have been unruly, and the accused would have had to listen to the "evidence"— most of it completely fabricated from superstition.

hanged on August 19, including Reverend George Burroughs. As he stood upon the platform of the gallows, he declared his innocence. Then he flawlessly recited the Lord's Prayer. This brought cries for mercy from the crowds. According to the account of a witness, Cotton Mather convinced the spectators that this was a trick played by the devil, and Burroughs was hanged.

Nine more accused witches died in September. Eight were hanged on September 22. Only three days before, Giles Corey, Martha's eighty-year-old husband, had been killed. When he had refused to enter a plea, the court had resorted to an English procedure meant to force prisoners to enter a plea so the trial could proceed. He was staked to the ground and a wooden plank placed on top of him. Stones were heaped on top of the plank, a few at a time, gradually increasing the weight. But he refused to plead guilty or innocent. He was finally crushed to death.

The trial of eighty-year-old Giles Corey. Corey refused to grant the trials legitimacy by entering a plea. When he refused, he was killed by having a plank placed on his chest and heavy stones added to it until he was crushed to death.

The Witch-Hunts End

With the prison overflowing and the number of afflicted now near fifty, the ministers in the colony grew more suspicious of spectral evidence. They finally took a stand against it, especially after some of the afflicted accused Lady Phips, the wife of the royal governor.

Cotton Mather and the other ministers had been mostly silent during the months of trials and hangings. In October, however, Increase Mather told the court, "It were better that ten suspected witches should escape, than that one innocent person should be condemned." He devoutly believed that witches must be destroyed, but the evidence must be "as clear as in any other crimes of a capital nature," he said.

Phips soon disbanded the court and organized a new court to complete the trials. Most of the accused were now acquitted. Eight were convicted and sentenced to death, but Phips granted reprieves

"There was an appearance that said, 'Kill the children. . . . ' Sometimes it is like a hog, and sometimes like a great dog . . . [or] a man with a yellow bird . . . [or] two rats, a red rat and a black rat."

Confession of Tituba, Salem, 1692

"Tituba's confession is in general similar to witchcraft confessions from other times and places. Part of it may have been suggested to her. But not all. It is far too detailed and far too original in some of its details to have been merely the product of the magistrate's leading questions."

Historian Chadwick Hansen, *Witchcraft at Salem*, 1969

to all of them. The court met for the last time on May 9, 1693, and all accused were acquitted that day, ending the witch hysteria in and around Salem.

The new skepticism about spectral evidence cast doubt on the convictions and executions that had occurred in the previous months. Had the state murdered innocent people? People who had participated in the witch trials soon began to admit that they had made errors of judgment. In January 1697, only five years after the events of Salem, the clergy declared an Official Day of Humiliation. By 1703, the colonial legislature began issuing pardons to the people who had been convicted and executed. In 1711, it also began compensating the families of the victims of the witch-hunts.

What Caused the Fits?

Many explanations have been given for the strange behavior of the "bewitched" girls. Some historians have assumed the girls were faking their problems. Life was harsh and strict. The alleged bewitchment allowed the girls to behave in ways that would have been severely punished under normal circumstances. They could get away with throwing Bibles, shouting, making outrageous statements about their elders, crawling on the floor, howling, and so on.

Nineteenth-century historian Charles W. Upham contended in an essay that the girls had shown "deliberate cunning and cool malice." Enjoying the power and attention, they perfected their performances. They then yielded to pressure to name those who had bewitched them. He wrote:

It was perhaps their original design to gratify a love of notoriety or of mischief by creating a sensation and excitement in their neighborhood, or, at the worst, to wreak their vengeance upon one or two individuals who had offended them. They soon, however, became intoxicated by the terrible success of their imposture, and were swept along by the frenzy they had occasioned.

History professor John Putnam Demos agrees in his book *Entertaining Satan.* He writes:

> The seizures of the afflicted children also permitted them to engage in a considerable amount of direct aggression. They were not, of course, held personally responsible; it was always the fault of the Devil at work inside them.

Not all historians believe the girls were simply rebelling or acting up. Some believe that by accusing others, the girls were trying to hide their own involvement with the occult. Other historians suggest that the girls truly thought they were possessed by the devil.

Biologist Linnda R. Caporael suggested another fascinating possibility in a 1976 issue of *Science* magazine. She blamed the girls' symptoms on

In this fanciful illustration, an accused witch in court causes a lightning bolt to come through a window.

74

convulsive ergotism. It was "once a common condition resulting from eating contaminated rye bread," she wrote. Ergot is a mold that can develop in grains, especially during damp, warm weather. Ergotism could cause convulsions, choking, headaches, depression, delirium, hallucinations, and crawling and tingling sensations in the skin, she reported. Other scientists, however, have disputed this theory.

Another theory suggests that one political/social faction was using the girls to rid Salem of another faction. The girls were pressed into service against the accused and kept in a highly emotional state. Their hysteria was real, but it was fed by the people of power and position who actually tried the cases and testified at the trials.

Mental Illness?

In a 1943 article in the *American Journal of Diseases of Children*, pediatrician and history enthusiast Ernest Caulfield said the children were obviously mentally ill. Confusion, conflict, and fear about their religion brought on the mental illness. Their ministers constantly reminded them that they were sinful simply because they were human and that they were likely doomed to eternal hell. Caulfield writes:

> They were sick children in the worst sort of mental distress—living in fear for their very lives and the welfare of their immortal souls. Hysteria was only the outward manifestation of their feeble attempts to escape from their insecure, cruel, depressive Salem Village world—a world thoroughly saturated with the pungent fumes of burning brimstone.

However, historian Marc Mappen asks why the same conditions did not trigger witch crazes among children in other New England towns.

These explanations of the children's "affliction" seem to assume that witchcraft was not actually a factor in the whole chain of events at Salem. But historian Chadwick Hansen suggests that some people actually were practicing witchcraft and magic. Like Caulfield, Hansen says the Salem girls were suffering from hysteria. But the hysteria was caused by the girls' fear of the workings of local witches. Hansen says Tituba was clearly practicing magic. He also lists others who dabbled in the occult and practiced evil witchcraft, including Bridget Bishop. Two laborers in Bishop's house testified they had found puppets behind a cellar wall. Bishop apparently used them for casting evil spells, since they were "made up of rags and hog's bristles, with headless pins in them."

Magic works because of fear and suggestion, Hansen says. The girls' fits were caused by the *fear* of magic rather than by the magic itself. People who know an evil spell has been cast upon them are likely to become sick if they believe magic can make them sick. The Puritans believed that witches could cause sickness and even death, and the afflicted girls were terrified.

Cotton Mather's Role

Through the centuries, Cotton Mather has been considered one of the major villains of the Salem witch-hunts. Mather vehemently believed that witches were wicked, even if they practiced white, or good, magic. Although Mather did counsel caution in trying the accused witches, he wanted to see all witches identified and punished. Mather maintained that the trials at Salem exposed the devil's plot against New England.

Like so many other aspects of this bleak period, Mather's role is also subject to debate. Some historians call him one of the fiercest of witch-hunters and hold him responsible for much of the hysteria and cruelty. But others claim he has been wrongly cast as the villain. He was a man of his time, they say. He was not being unduly cruel or overeager to cast stones at his fellow citizens. He was seeing that

Cotton Mather's role in the Salem witch trials continues to be evaluated by historians. Opinions of him range from relentless religious fanatic to the one who stopped the trials with his doubt.

The title page of Cotton Mather's book. Did Mather use the witch trials to prevent non-Puritans from gaining equal footing with citizens who were Puritans? Were the witch trials a result of religious intolerance?

The Wonders of the Invisible World:

Being an Account of the

TRYALS

OF

Several Witches,

Lately Excuted in

NEW-ENGLAND:

And of several remarkable Curiosities therein Occurring.

Together with,

I. Observations upon the Nature, the Number, and the Operations of the Devils.

II. A short Narrative of a late outrage committed by a knot of Witches in Swede-Land, very much resembling, and so far explaining, that under which New-England has laboured.

III. Some Councels directing a due Improvement of the Terrible things lately done by the unusual and amazing Range of Evil-Spirits in New-England.

IV. A brief Discourse upon those Temptations which are the more ordinary Devices of Satan.

By COTTON MATHER.

Published by the Special Command of his EXCELLENCY the Govencur of the Province of the Massachusetts-Bay in New-England.

Printed first, at Boston in New-England; and Reprinted at London, for John Dunton, at the Raven in the Paultry. 1693.

God's work was done and that the devil was defeated. Mather actually was a voice of reason and caution, according to Hansen.

But was he a religious fanatic, or was he self-serving? Did he really serve God, or was he part of a conspiracy? Historian Enders Robinson suggests that a small group of men in Salem Village actually started the witch-hunts as a personal vendetta to destroy their enemies. Robinson says the hunt was not aimed at the poor or downtrodden. It was aimed at "mothers, wives, and daughters in the upper eche-lons of society, rich widows and respectable matrons, army officers and sea captains, wealthy merchants and large landholders, and ministers and church members."

Robinson writes in his book *The Devil Discovered* that ten men formed the conspiracy. Parris and Thomas Putnam were the most conspicuous, but their power came from higher authorities, including Cotton Mather and other ministers, judges, magis-trates, and officials. This Puritan "old guard" hated and feared the new royal charter. Under the old char-ter Massachusetts had been a Puritan commonwealth. The new charter promised greater democracy and religious freedom to non-Puritans. It threatened the power and authority of the Puritan old guard that had ruled the colony since the 1620s. Robinson sug-gests that this group of powerful men "subtly encouraged superstition and prejudice. . . . They urged forward the witchcraft persecutions in a des-perate attempt to retain the power of their old Puritan theocracy." (A theocracy is a state or country ruled by religious authority.)

Witchcraft trials and executions were part of the fabric of life in Puritan New England. To the

A witch-hunt in Salem. As surprising as it seems to us, the Puritans avidly believed in witches and the devil as a constant and real threat. Unexplained deaths, poor crops, and unusual weather needed to be explained, and, to the unscientific, witchcraft seemed as logical an explanation as any.

Puritans, witchcraft was more about pacts with the devil than it was about magic. But it was also part of God's divine plan—He both allowed and opposed this intrusion by the devil. Can the people of Salem and the colony at large be condemned for accepting a commonly held belief of the day? *Not believing in witchcraft would have been more shocking.*

When any ill befell the community or an individual, the people of Puritan New England looked closely for reasons. Witchcraft was always a possibility, although usually a particular person was suspected rather than witchcraft in general. Cotton Mather considered the witch-hunts and trials an entirely proper response to rid the area of witches. But Robert Calef, one of his chief critics, wrote in 1697 in a book entitled *More Wonders of the Invisible World* that the trials themselves, rather than witchcraft, were the real evil.

A "Perfectly Natural Superstition"

George Lyman Kittredge, an early twentieth-century historian, viewed the Salem witch-hunt "not as an abnormal outbreak of fanaticism, not as an isolated tragedy, but as a mere incident, a brief and transitory episode in the biography of a terrible, but perfectly natural, superstition." Belief in witches was part of the Puritan religion; putting witches to death was an acceptable and expected punishment, said Kittredge. He even made the case that the New Englanders had shown great restraint compared to Europeans who had executed hundreds of thousands. He chastised critics of the Salem authorities: "It is easy to be wise after the fact, especially when the fact is two hundred years old."

The loss of the charter may have egged on the people of Salem, some historians say. They had founded the colony as a covenant with God. The loss of the charter meant they must have sinned against God and against their covenant; the witch-craft outbreak was further proof that sin was rampant.

Another reason often cited for the Salem witch-craft hysteria was politics. Salem Village was teetering on the brink of disaster in 1692, say historians Paul Boyer and Stephen Nissenbaum in their book *Salem Possessed.* Tension, caused by the villagers' resentment of the townspeople, was ready to erupt. The townspeople were more sophisticated and generally wealthier, while the villagers remained more agricultural. A majority of the afflicted girls who made the accusations were from village families, while a majority of the accused were citizens of Salem Town. Boyer and Nissenbaum write:

> The problems which confronted Salem Village in fact encompassed some of the central issues of New England society in the late seventeenth century: the resistance of back-country farmers to the pressures of commercial capitalism and the social style that accompanied it; the breaking away of outlying areas from parent towns; difficulties between ministers and their congregations; the crowding of third-generation sons from family lands . . . the very quality of life in an unsettled age.

Even within Salem Village, the people were divided into two factions, the pro-Parris group (the primary witch accusers, led by the Putnam family) and the anti-Parris group (the anti-witch-hunt group led by the Porter family). Boyer and Nissenbaum show that the split was fairly consistent along lines of wealth and residence. The part of Salem Village that was a stronghold of anti-Parris sentiment also seemed to be much wealthier than the pro-Parris faction, according to tax records.

Crimes Against Women

It is no coincidence that most of the accused witches were females, say some historians. Carol Karlsen, historian and author of *The Devil in the Shape of a Woman*, writes, "Only by understanding

"I am falsely accused."

Sarah Good, accused and convicted of being a witch, Salem, 1692

"[Sarah Good's] answers were in a very wicked, spiteful manner, reflecting and retorting against the authority with base and abusive words and many lies . . . . It was said that her husband said that he was afraid that she was either a witch or would be one very quickly."

A clerk at Sarah Good's trial, 1692

A witch trial. Some scholars believe witch trials were based upon a hatred of women—especially atypical women who refused to obey their husbands, or those who had no husbands, or the worst—those who seemed to be able to live outside the confines of marriage.

that the history of witchcraft is primarily a history of women . . . can we confront the deeply imbedded feelings about women . . . among our witch-ridden ancestors."

Salem men were the heirs to the views of women set forth in the *Malleus Maleficarum*: women were seen as chattel (property), sinners, and inferiors to men in moral, spiritual, and intellectual matters. Women were tempters and easily tempted, vulnerable to the workings of evil and the allure of the devil.

Order and hierarchy were of utmost importance to the Puritans, says Karlsen. That order called for men to be the heads of households and leaders of the church and the community. A woman was supposed to live under the authority of a male—if not her husband, then her father, brother, or master of the household in which she was a servant. Karlsen observes that the witch-hunts started in New England when this social order was threatened, when woman's subservience to man was challenged: the population of women without men had become significant, and many widows inherited or stood to inherit land. The number of women beyond child-bearing age was increasing, as well.

According to historian Selma Williams, in her book *Riding the Nightmare*:

> Woman, the conspicuous incarnation of evil, was the obvious scapegoat—especially if she attracted attention against the established order, or by disturbing the natural setup in any way—or if she was past her ability to bear children, her sole contribution to society and the only justification for allowing her to share man's hard-won food, clothing, and shelter in the first place.

Statistics may bear out these theories that the Salem witch-hunt was based on misogyny because 141 of the 185 people accused of witchcraft during the Salem witch-hunts were women. Twenty-six of the thirty-one convicted were women. Fourteen of the nineteen executed for witchcraft in Salem were women. Most of the men who were implicated were relatives of the accused women.

To the Puritans, their world order was the order that God had decreed. Any attempt to disrupt the status quo was obviously the work of the devil—and women were, without a doubt, his allies.

After Salem, accusations of witchcraft in colonial New England were rare. If men and women practiced witchcraft, they practiced it secretly. In the latter half of the twentieth century, however, it would resurface—not as devil worship but as a new pagan religion, often with a goddess as its deity.

"Is it possible that the practice of witchcraft was one of the very few ways in which a woman could impress herself on a male chauvinist world, at a time when economic opportunities were limited, the structure of the family was changing only very slowly, and when feminine eroticism was strongly condemned?"

History professor Lawrence Stone, *The New York Review of Books*, December 12, 1971

"Witchcraft in colonial New England meant more than women's refusal to subordinate themselves to men with institutional authority over them: it suggested their refusal to subordinate themselves to all persons whom God had placed above them in the social hierarchy."

Historian Carol F. Karlsen, *The Devil in the Shape of a Woman*, 1987

Four

Do You Know Any Witches?

In basements, meadows, and city parks, men and women meet. They cast a circle, purifying a space for ritual. They invoke the four compass directions and the four elements of earth, water, air, and fire. They join hands around the circle and dance, slowly at first, then faster and faster. They chant words of power and words of magic. The cone of power is raised, shimmering with energy above the circle.

The people at this ritual are witches. Maybe you have met a witch and did not even know it. Today, many people in modern cultures consider themselves witches. Since the 1950s, witchcraft and magic have resurfaced. Perhaps the interest is part of a search for spirituality and reconnection with nature.

What Is Contemporary Witchcraft?

To many contemporary witches, witchcraft is simply "the Craft." It is the practice of sorcery—simple folk magic and healing work. Some of these witches say they learned the Craft from their families, where it had been passed on through generations, perhaps for centuries. They call themselves "family tradition" witches. Some family tradition witches and other witches consider themselves "natural" because they have strong psychic (mental

and spiritual) powers that strengthen their magical abilities.

Neopagans

To many witches, witchcraft is a religion just as Judaism, Christianity, Buddhism, Islam, Hinduism, and other belief systems are religions. These witches consider themselves neopagans (*neo* means "new"). Many neopagan witches prefer to call themselves Wiccans, since the word does not carry the negative associations that the word *witchcraft* does. Wiccans may also call their religion the Old Religion because they trace their beliefs to the pagan nature-based religions that predated Christianity in Europe. Although they practice magic and magical rituals, their emphasis is on worship of the ancient deities, especially the Goddess (the supreme god as a female, the mother of all), rather than on magic. Their rites and rituals are based on the cycles of nature—for example, the seasons and the phases of the moon.

Modern witchcraft, like earlier witchcraft, is shrouded in secrecy. Estimating the numbers who practice witchcraft, either as a craft or a religion, is nearly impossible. But anthropologists say witchcraft has a small but growing following. Some estimates say the number of neopagan witches in the United States is between ten thousand and fifty thousand.

The majority of American witches are probably white, middle-class women. Some authorities believe this is because witchcraft tends to honor the Goddess. Major Western religions suppressed the feminine aspect of the divine and portrayed God as entirely male. Therefore, many women have been drawn to a religion that worships a female deity.

Witches say that most of the public does not understand witchcraft today. They are disturbed by critics who claim that witches are satanists who

practice evil magic and cause harm. Witches say that their craft or religion has nothing to do with satanism; witches have no relationship with the devil. Their religion existed long before Christianity and Christianity's concept of the devil. Rather than believing in evil and destruction, they say, contemporary witchcraft reveres nature and all living things. They assert that their magic and rituals are intended to bring harmony, not harm.

Modern witches pose with their children. Today, those who call themselves witches worship nature as a goddess and practice many of the ancient healing arts.

Worshipping the Goddess and Horned God

Although witches may worship many pagan nature deities, the chief deity of most neopagan witches is the Goddess. The Goddess is associated with the moon and is worshipped in her three aspects. These correspond to three goddesses and three stages of life represented by the moon's phases: Diana, the maiden, associated with the new moon; Selene, the mother, associated with the full moon; and Hecate, the crone (or old woman), associated with the waning moon.

Worship of a goddess dates back ten thousand to thirty-five thousand years, according to some scholars. They suggest that the first agricultural societies worshipped a goddess as their primary deity. Goddess worship flourished in the Mediterranean region, especially between 1500 B.C. and 900 B.C. According to some sources, goddess-worshipping cults continued in parts of Europe even during the Middle Ages. Many cults centered on Diana, the Roman goddess of the moon and the hunt.

Healing the Planet

Worship of the Goddess may not have any historical link with medieval witchcraft. But witches say their revival of Goddess-worship is a celebration of the power of women and the importance of female energy in healing the planet. To many witches, the Goddess is not a supernatural being. She is a symbol of the creative force, nature, and female energy. (According to witches and many other schools of thought, all people—men and women—have both male and female energy.)

Some neopagan witches also worship a chief male deity, the Horned God, the Goddess's male partner or mate. The Horned God's origins also may date back to Paleolithic times. He was known by many different names, including Pan (Greek god of woodlands), Janus (Roman god of good beginnings), Dionysus (Greek god of wine), and Cernunnos (Celtic god of fertility, animals, and the underworld). His horns symbolize the woodlands and the crescent moon. According to some theories, the witches of the burning times were actually worshipping the Horned God, not Satan, when they gathered for their sabbats. The Horned God was not associated with the devil. To today's witches, the Horned God represents the masculine energy that both men and women have.

The Wiccan Rede

Ethics are also an important part of contemporary witchcraft. Most witches, both followers of the Craft and the Old Religion, adhere to a basic moral creed: "An if it harm none, do what ye will." These words are known as the Wiccan Rede. (*Rede* comes from the Old English word *roedan* meaning "to guide or direct." *An* is short for "and.")

The origins of the Wiccan Rede are unknown. It may have roots in centuries-old tradition. But it may have been coined in the twentieth century by Gerald Gardner, known as the father of modern witchcraft, to combat the image of witch as evildoer. Some witches believe that the effort to combat the evil-witch image has inhibited their effectiveness. They say the Rede has been interpreted so narrowly that they have been prevented from cursing those who should be cursed!

Witches disagree on the limits the Rede imposes. Most witches believe that they should not interfere

Modern witches meet in Mexico City and participate in a ritual to ask Mother Earth for forgiveness for humanity's crimes against her. Most modern witches protest the evil crone image, insisting that their practices, by oath, must work toward good in the world.

with the choices of others, and they should not cast any spells that might harm or manipulate anyone. Some believe they should not cast any spell without the permission of those who would be directly affected. These witches, for example, do not direct love spells towards attracting a particular person. Instead the spells are intended to attract "the right partner."

Some witches interpret the Wiccan Rede to mean that they must not cast spells against wrongdoers, even murderers. Instead, they must cast spells to protect potential victims. But some witches cast "binding" spells to prevent evil acts, or to cause wrongdoers to bring about their own downfall. For example, a binding spell against a criminal might call for the criminal to make mistakes that will lead to his or her arrest. If witches follow the Rede strictly, they cast spells that bring about solutions that benefit all, rather than casting spells *against* anyone.

Witches also cast spells to bring about healing for the planet and its inhabitants, focusing on environmental issues and world peace.

Many witches also subscribe to a belief in personal responsibility for their own actions. They believe that "What good you do returns to you threefold; what harm you do also returns to you threefold." This belief is based on the Eastern law of "karma" or cause and effect: good brings good in return, and evil brings evil in return.

Magic and the Supernatural

Witches in antiquity and in native cultures called upon the supernatural in order to perform magic. But how do magic and the supernatural fit into the belief system of today's scientifically knowledgeable witch?

Isaac Bonewits, a magician and neopagan priest, is quoted in *Drawing Down the Moon* by Margot Adler as saying that magic is "a combination of an art and a science that is designed to enable people to make effective use of their psychic talents." He explains that the only difference between magic and science is that magic "deals with a body of knowledge that, for one reason or another, has not yet been fully investigated or confirmed by the other arts and sciences."

Developing Natural Powers

Magic is the ability to use one's intuition and psychic and mental abilities to achieve a particular result. (Intuition is the ability to sense or know something automatically; some people call it an inner knowing.) Many witches are highly psychic and intuitive. Through practice they learn to direct and control their powers. Wiccan practice is intended to develop the natural powers of all who participate. Witches believe that all people have some level of psychic ability and can be trained to use it to direct their wills towards individual and group goals.

Most witches dismiss the idea of the supernatural as a source of power. They contend that there is no such thing as the supernatural because there is nothing that can be outside of nature. Adler quotes witch Mark Roberts: "In our workings we have achieved and produced nothing supernatural: we have simply reached our level of natural capacity." Witch Leo Martello, author of *Witchcraft: The Old Religion*, writes: "I make no claims as a witch to 'supernatural powers,' but I totally believe in the *super* powers that reside in the *natural*." In other words, most witches today believe that they draw their power from the awesome forces of nature.

Laurie Cabot, who had herself proclaimed "the official witch of Salem [Massachusetts]," says she sees no contradiction between witchcraft and science. In fact, she teaches that witchcraft *is* a science. She says magical spells are step-by-step experiments that

"I should be surprised if nobody has put forward a theory that would make witchcraft the last degenerate trace of the spiritual sciences that came to us from lost Atlantis."

History professor Elliot Rose, *A Razor for a Goat*, 1989

"We must bear in mind that in a society which believes in witchcraft, it works."

Historian Chadwick Hansen, *Witchcraft at Salem*, 1969

produce measurable results. She writes in her book *Power of the Witch:*

> Many people still think that science and magic are opposed to each other, science being hard, practical, real, and magic being soft, fanciful, and imaginary. Yet nothing could be further from the truth. To the wise, to Witches versed and trained in the old ways of our ancestors, magic and science are equal threads of power, woven through the same fabric of life. Magic and the natural sciences are allies, and together make up the science of witchcraft.

Cabot's teaching explains how and why magic works, based on the teachings of modern physics:

> Witch's consciousness can effect changes in the physical world (or mental and emotional worlds) because, based on what we know from subatomic experiments, *what* we see and *how* what we see behaves depends on our participation, our effort, our involvement. . . . The human mind is truly powerful because it is a participator, not a mere observer and recorder.

The Practice of Magic

Witches today may practice several kinds of magic. They may divine (read the future) through use of astrology, crystal balls, runes, or tarot cards. The tarot is a deck of seventy-eight picture cards. Runes are magical symbols dating back to the Saxons, Norse, Danes, and Vikings during the Middle Ages. Witches also may know how to use herbs, image magic, spell casting, incantations, or potions.

Most witches say magic is the ability to direct one's will towards a desired result. It works because of psychic energy, strong belief, or will power. English witch Doreen Valiente says, "The mind is the greatest instrument of magic." When witches get together, they use their combined energy to achieve results. They say that a group of people focusing on the same outcome produces a large amount of energy, which creates more likelihood of success. Some people might say that visualization, a technique used by mental health and motivation experts, among others, is a form of magic. Visualizations involve the practice of concentrating on an outcome and picturing it as if it has already happened. Many mental health experts today recommend that people use visualizations to help them reach their goals. Star athletes, especially, visualize success in their sports events—does that mean they are using magic?

Writer and witch Scott Cunningham points out in *The Truth About Witchcraft Today*, "The magic is in the magician, not within the tools. . . . Spells are designed to release personal power within the magician. It is this energy—along with natural objects such as crystals, herbs, oils, incense, and the like— that powers the spells, that gets it moving."

Witches believe their spells have power. But skeptics say that when spells work, it is only coincidence. Some critics caution that spells are dangerous—not because they work but because they are "pagan." These critics mistakenly believe *pagan* means backward and evil. Some still equate magic and witchcraft with the devil, and they fear that magic spells will open the door to Satan. They are correct when they claim that "witchcraft is not Christian." But neither is it anti-Christian, witches point out; witchcraft lies outside established religious tradition. Witches, however, are open to a variety of spiritual influences.

Witch Laurie Cabot sees no contradiction between her practices and science. She believes that magic and science are two pieces to the puzzle of the universe.

Wiccan Religious Ritual

Witches say their rituals and magic are a means of making contact with mysterious forces and energies—both within humans and in the universe—to bring about strength, unity, and benefit to all.

Wiccans worship alone or in small groups. Many say there is nothing magical about the number thirteen for a coven; a coven can be two or three people, or fifty. But twelve or thirteen is a large enough group to generate energy and small enough to work efficiently. Some witches say thirteen is a good number for the practical reason that the traditional nine-foot circle would be too crowded with more than thirteen people!

Casting a Circle: Establishing a Sacred Space and Time

Casting a circle is one of the first orders of business in Wiccan ritual, whether working alone or in a coven. The circle is drawn in the air and may also be outlined on the ground. The circle symbolizes wholeness, the womb, the cycles of life, and the seasons. Only after the circle has been cast and the space purified can any other ritual begin. Casting a circle establishes a sacred space and time for all rites, magic, and healing work. "The circle (sphere) of energy is the Wiccan temple," writes Scott Cunningham, a practicing Wiccan. It is a place for ritual and worship, like a chapel, church, or synagogue. In some traditions, the space is swept with a broom to symbolically rid it of negative energy before the circle is cast.

In casting the circle, the spirits or energies of the four directions and the four elements are invoked. Inside the circle, the physical and the spiritual meet; it is a place of great power, trust, and energy. An altar with ritual objects is set up within the circle. The sacred objects include candles, a wand, a chalice, salt, flowers, and a pentacle. The pentacle is a five-pointed star with religious and magical importance to witches and magicians. In witchcraft rituals, the pentacle is a metal, clay, or wax disk with a star inscribed on it.

Inside the circle, the individual or group "raises the cone of power." That is, through music, dancing, and chanting, the group raises and releases the psychic energy needed to bring about healing or to focus on some other goal.

"Drawing Down the Moon" and the Ritual Dance of Witches

One of the many important rituals that may be practiced is that known as "drawing down the

moon." In this ritual, the high priestess goes into a trance and the Goddess is invoked, or drawn down into the priestess so that she becomes the Goddess.

Dance is an important part of Wiccan ritual, as dance and chanting have been used by primitive cultures for centuries to reach an altered consciousness. While in an altered state, an individual is more open to magic and the spirit world. Dancing together enhances the combined power of the individuals. It raises the energy of the group and enables it to work magic together.

After ritual worship and magic have been completed, the circle is released. The priest or priestess

The rituals of modern-day witches resemble those observed by pre-Christians. Here, Joyce Seigrist, High Priestess of the Rosegate Coven of Rhode Island, extinguishes the candles at the end of a religious ceremony called the circle.

might walk around the circle, using a wand to undo the circle and return the space to everyday use.

Esbat and Sabbat

Most modern witches celebrate eight major festivals during the year. They are rooted in pagan celebration of the natural cycles governed by movements of the sun, moon, and earth.

Four of the festivals, called sabbats, occur at the equinoxes and solstices. Equinoxes are the two times of year when day and night are of equal lengths in all parts of the earth. Solstices are the times when the sun is at its southernmost or northernmost points. Yule, on December 20 or 21, celebrates the winter solstice. Ostara, on March 20 or 21, celebrates the spring equinox. Midsummer, the summer solstice, is June 21. Harvestide, the autumn equinox, is September 20 or 21.

The other four witch feasts are Imbolc, Beltane, Lammas, and Samhain. Imbolc (or Oimelc), celebrated February 1 or 2, was a pagan winter purification and fire festival commemorating the end of winter darkness and the return of the first rays of light. It also became a minor Christian holiday—and coincides with Groundhog Day.

Beltane, on April 30, the eve of May Day, is a festival of birth, fertility, and the renewal of life. It includes celebration around the maypole, a symbol of fertility. Lammas (or Lughnasadh), on August 1, is a festival of games, dance, and first harvest. Samhain, on October 31, celebrates the beginning of winter. It is the time when the veil between the worlds of the living and the dead is at its thinnest, allowing contact with the spirit world to be made more easily. It coincides with the Christian All Hallow's Eve or Halloween.

Most pagan festivals coincide with Christian or Western holidays and traditions because the church adopted them to hasten the conversion of pagans to Christianity. The winter solstice, for example, has

For witches, Halloween celebrates the beginning of winter and a time when spirits may be contacted more easily. Here, Diedre Pulgram and Andras Corban pose behind an altar in their attic as they prepare to perform rituals to honor dead relatives and friends on Halloween.

been Christianized as Christmas. The spring equinox coincides with Easter. Many covens also meet at each full moon or more often.

The Growth of Witchcraft

Is contemporary witchcraft the remnant of an ancient religion or a recent invention? Margot Adler says the Wiccan revival "starts with a myth." That myth goes something like this: Witchcraft dates back to Paleolithic times when people worshipped the goddess of fertility and the god of the hunt. This early religion was universal, although the names of the gods varied from place to place. Christianity slowly took hold in Europe. So-called pagans and heathens clung to the old ways, so the church built its cathedrals on the pagans' sacred sites. It changed the names of pagan holidays but kept the same dates. Pagans changed some of their ways to make them acceptable to the authorities, who were Christian.

While the church destroyed or absorbed some traditions, other traditions went underground. Through the centuries, families across Europe and in remote areas of the United States and Canada continued to practice some of these ancient traditions. In 1951, when England's anti-witchcraft laws were revoked, witchcraft began to resurface there.

Adler says that at this point, the myth flies off in various directions, with each sect telling a different story of its roots. Many, however, credit the work of Margaret Murray, Robert Graves, Gerald Gardner, and other writers and anthropologists with reviving their ancient traditions.

The Father of Modern Witchcraft

To many, Gerald Gardner is the father of modern witchcraft. In the late 1930s, Gardner, an English civil servant, was initiated into a coven by its high priestess, Old Dorothy Clutterbuck. This coven claimed that its origins dated back to an ancient tradition that had survived the witch-hunts. Although its existence had remained secret even into the twentieth century, other covens were also said to be scattered across England and parts of Europe. In 1951, Gardner broke from the coven to start his own. Although he borrowed from the ritual of his original coven, he added much of his own ceremony, based on folklore, mythology, and literature, and perhaps the works of other occultists.

The Importance of the Goddess

Concerned that witchcraft would die out if he did not write about it, he published a novel and two nonfiction books. Although Gardner drew heavily from Murray's work, Gardner emphasized the importance of the Goddess rather than the Horned God. Some historians suggest that interest in goddess worship increased after World War II because people were looking for a way to save the world from a path of destruction. The Goddess has long been associated with nature and the celebration of life. And to many people seeking a new spirituality in the wake of a world war, the male God stands for domination—power over others—and that only leads to war and technology that kills.

Writer Margaret Murray was responsible for documenting and researching ancient witch practices. Many credit her with the modern-day witch craze.

Gardnerian covens spread. As the Goddess became the primary deity, the High Priestess, rather than the High Priest, became the coven leader.

New Traditions

Eventually, people broke from Gardnerian covens to start their own traditions. These various traditions were named for their founders or for their type of practice: Gardnerian, Alexandrian, Dianic, feminist, and so on.

Other witches also surfaced, claiming older or different traditions than those of Gardner. When Adler interviewed family-tradition witches, they told of hundreds of scattered traditions supposedly rooted in folk magic and in pagan belief, but as far as an organized religion that linked them all—there was none.

One witch told Adler that her grandmother never called herself a witch. She simply called her magic "having the power," and her craft was a religion of hearth and fireside. "Her beliefs were pagan, although her room was full of Roman Catholic statues and pictures," says Adler.

Adler quoted another witch, who told her, "My family used the word 'Witch' rather loosely for anyone who practiced 'magic.'"

Family-tradition witches have adapted with the times, Isaac Bonewits says, so it is impossible to sort out which traditions were handed down and which were adapted from other more modern sources. As one witch told Adler, "My mother taught me a few things. But maybe she got them out of the blue! Who knows if she got these from *her* grandmother." Witch Gwydion Pendderwen told Adler, "What has come down is so minimal, it could be thrown out without missing it."

Many scholars have dismissed contemporary witchcraft as a hodgepodge of myths and magic of questionable sources. But witches do not seem too concerned with the historical basis of their practice.

They say their witchcraft's origins may be questionable, but a spiritual continuity exists through the fragments of folklore, magic, and nature-centered and goddess-centered worship that survived.

Witches today, in fact, stress the importance of creating new rituals that are relevant to modern life. According to Adler, "Its real sources lie in the mind, in art, in creative work." One witch told Adler, "If the Fam-Trads have a law, that law should be: 'If it works, do it; if not, throw it out.' The Craft has always borrowed from every culture we've come in contact with."

Historian Elliot Rose, however, criticizes witchcraft's "shape-shifting." He writes in his book *A Razor for a Goat:*

> Perhaps there is some truth after all in the belief that witches can change their shapes. Witchcraft, as I believe, has changed its shape until it has no true shape left. Pursuing a phantom hope, how should it not follow wherever that hope might seem to stray? How could its footing be other than marshy, or its vision clear of vapours, when a jack-o'-lantern was its guiding light?

Critics Call Witchcraft Nonsense—or Worse

Witchcraft's critics condemn it for different reasons: some call witchcraft antiscientific nonsense, while others call it anti-Christian devil worship.

Some critics seem to accept the definition of witchcraft as a nature religion or a pagan religion. But they consider the practice to be escapist nonsense. They say people who flock to pagan practices are immature, or they are trying to escape the rational, scientific world in favor of superstition or nature worship. Some critics describe members of pagan or occult groups as selfish. They say that most of the people in these movements are absorbed in finding themselves, rather than working for change that benefits the poor and minorities.

"The witchcraze is an important study in human evil, comparable to Nazism and Stalinism in the present century."

Historian Jeffery B. Russell, *A History of Witchcraft,* 1980

"The Science of Magick is not evil, for by the knowledge of it, evill may bee eschewed, and good means thereof may be followed."

Scholar and philosopher Albertus Magnus, thirteenth century

As witches protest for civil rights, members of Christian churches march side by side to protest *them*. Many Christians still fear witches and believe that they are aligned with the devil.

But most critics of witchcraft denounce the practice on religious grounds. They insist that witchcraft is a form of devil worship. Television talk shows featuring discussion of witchcraft inevitably ask witches to share the stage with their most outspoken critics from fundamentalist Christian groups. These antiwitchcraft spokespersons blame witchcraft for much of the violence in society, and they claim that Satan and his servants are masterminding a conspiracy to take over the world.

The U.S. Constitution protects witchcraft and other neopagan organizations that identify themselves as religious organizations. In Canada, Wicca received legal recognition as a religion in 1987 after a witch brought a religious discrimination suit against his employer. Despite legal recognition, however, witches in North America have been combating the negative image they inherited from the days of the Inquisition.

The Media and the Current Image of Witches

The view of the evil witch is a common one that is often kept alive by movies, television talk shows, books, comedians, ministers, and even politicians. In 1985, two members of the U. S. Congress introduced bills to exclude neopagan and witchcraft organizations from tax-exempt status as religious groups. These politicians and their supporters had argued that witchcraft and other practices were harmful and did not deserve to be supported by a tax exemption. Both measures were defeated, but the attitude behind the movement continues. Many fundamentalist Christians consider witchcraft a threat to Christianity and to Western values and morality. They say that witchcraft, paganism, and the practice of magic have no place in the United States. In Arkansas in 1993, two witches ran into that same fear and prejudice that has dogged witches for centuries. They had opened a small bookshop but lost their lease when the landlord and local ministers found out that they sold books on witchcraft, incense, wands, and other Wiccan tools.

Practicing witches say that they wish people could understand that witches are not evil, do not worship the devil, and are ordinary people who practice a non-Christian religion. They are frustrated that critics misinterpret their traditions. Margot Adler writes, "The feeling persists that those who practice Witchcraft or occultism [supernatural practices] are engaged in something fearful. . . . This image has a long history. It is nourished by the media because it sells. But more

Many today continue to fear and abhor witchcraft, even though modern-day witches claim to be completely benign. Here protesters march outside a public library where a self-proclaimed witch lectures on her faith.

important, this image encourages a fear of the unknown that blunts most people's curiosity and adventurousness."

What Makes a Witch a Witch?

Modern witchcraft bears little resemblance to the witchcraft described in Inquisition records. Modern witchcraft claims some roots in the paganism of long ago, but it is a spiritual link more than a historical link. Then what makes today's witch a witch? What connects these people called "witches" through the ages?

Witches say they are connected to a natural power that is timeless and universal. Their existence reminds us that magic may really exist, available to all of us. They are in touch with the mystery that underlies our reality. In essence, maybe it is simply mystery that links witches down through the centuries.

Conclusion

The Mystery Remains

Even in this rational world with its scientific beliefs, few people remain neutral when they hear the word *witch* or meet someone who claims to practice witchcraft. Witches still bring out a gut-level emotional response. People still consider them "different," and "otherworldly." Witches appear on talk shows, and viewers still whisper, "She said she's a witch! I didn't think witches existed!" Or, "I don't believe in that stuff. But I sure wouldn't want to make her mad!" At best they might think of witches as exotic or eccentric. At worst, they might think of them as satanists, child killers, or a threat to Christianity.

No matter how much we read about the historical basis of the witch-hunts or the spiritual tradition of the witch, witches remain a mystery. The witches of the Middle Ages and Renaissance remain mysterious because the truth about their alleged evil was lost in the flames that destroyed them. We will never really know if they were devil worshippers, or pagans, or simply midwives, healers, and folk magicians. We are left only with the records of the Inquisition—the institution that tried and executed them—and with images from fairy tales and art.

No matter how harmless modern-day witches seem or the more society finds out about the false accusations of witches past, the evil archetype of the witch continues to haunt our dreams and our unconscious. The power of the witch as symbol—the embodiment of evil, preying on the good and the innocent—is still very much alive.

Witches today are a mystery because they claim a faith that is tens of thousands of years old, and they honor a deity in female form. They believe in nature spirits *and* science. They believe in the supernatural *and* human potential and the power of the mind.

Perhaps we need witches in our world, especially today. Perhaps we are fascinated and threatened by witches because they remind us that there are no simple answers to the wonders of the universe or the atrocities of history. Witches continue to keep the flames of mystery burning, and it is mystery that feeds our curiosity and keeps our minds and our hearts open. Mystery stirs us to look for answers that lead to still more questions.

For Further Exploration

Rhoda Blumberg, *Witches*. New York: Franklin Watts, 1979.

Scott Cunningham, *The Truth About Witchcraft Today*. St. Paul, MN: Llewellyn Publications, 1988.

Rosemary Ellen Guiley, *The Encyclopedia of Witches and Witchcraft*. New York: Facts on File, 1989.

Carol F. Karlsen, *The Devil in the Shape of a Woman*. New York: Norton, 1987.

Bernice Kohn, *Out of the Cauldron: A Short History of Witchcraft*. New York: Holt, Rinehart & Winston, 1972.

Georgess McHargue, *Meet the Witches*. New York: Lippincott, 1984.

Derek Parker and Julia Parker, *The Power of Magic*. New York: Simon & Schuster, 1992.

Marion L. Starkey, *The Devil in Massachusetts: Witchcraft in Colonial New England*. Garden City, NY: Anchor Books, Doubleday, 1949, 1969.

Selma R. Williams and Pamela Williams Adelman, *Riding the Nightmare: Women & Witchcraft*. New York: HarperCollins, 1978.

Additional Works Consulted

Margot Adler, *Drawing Down the Moon: Witches, Druids, Goddess-Worshippers, and Other Pagans in America Today*. Boston: Beacon Press, 1979, 1986.

Laurie Cabot, *Power of the Witch: The Earth, the Moon, and the Magical Path to Enlightenment*. New York: Bantam Doubleday Dell, 1989.

John Putnam Demos, *Entertaining Satan: Witchcraft and the Culture of Early New England*. Oxford: Oxford University Press, 1982.

Gerald Gardner, *Witchcraft Today*. New York: Magickal Childe Publishing, 1954, 1991.

Chadwick Hansen, *Witchcraft at Salem*. New York: George Braziller, 1969.

Erica Jong, *Witches*. New York: Harry N. Abrams, 1981.

Marc Mappen, ed., *Witches & Historians: Interpretations of Salem*. Malabar, FL: Robert E. Krieger, 1980.

Margaret A. Murray, *The God of the Witches*. Oxford: Oxford University Press, 1931, 1970.

Enders A. Robinson, *The Devil Discovered: Salem Witchcraft 1692*. New York: Hippocrene Books, 1991.

Elliot Rose, *A Razor for a Goat*. Toronto: University of Toronto Press, 1989.

Jeffrey B. Russell, *A History of Witchcraft: Sorcerers, Heretics, and Pagans*. London: Thames and Hudson, 1980.

Index

About the Author

Wendy Stein, a freelance writer and editor, lives in Pompey, New York. She has written and edited materials on a variety of subjects, including health, social studies, history, consumer education, and communication skills. She has written four *Great Mysteries: Opposing Viewpoints: Atlantis, Shamans, Dinosaurs*, and *Witches*. Her other books include: *Taking the Wheel; Ready, Set, Study;* and *Communication Skills That Work.*

She earned a B.A. in English and religion from Trinity College in Hartford, Connecticut, and an M.A. in public communications from Syracuse University.

She enjoys canoeing, camping, and whale watching.

Picture Credits